DNA
INVESTIGATIONS

TRUE CRIME FROM WHARNCLIFFE

Foul Deeds and Suspicious Deaths Series

Barking, Dagenham & Chadwell Heath
Barnsley
Bath
Bedford
Birmingham
More Foul Deeds Birmingham
Black Country
Blackburn and Hyndburn
Bolton
Bradford
Brighton
Bristol
Cambridge
Carlisle
Chesterfield
Cumbria
More Foul Deeds Chesterfield
Colchester
Coventry
Croydon
Derby
Durham
Ealing
Fens
Folkstone and Dover
Grimsby
Guernsey
Guildford
Halifax
Hampstead, Holborn and St Pancras
Huddersfield

Hull
Jersey
Leeds
Leicester
Lewisham and Deptford
Liverpool
London's East End
London's West End
Manchester
Mansfield
More Foul Deeds Wakefield
Newcastle
Newport
Norfolk
Northampton
Nottingham
Oxfordshire
Pontefract and Castleford
Portsmouth
Rotherham
Scunthorpe
Sheffield
Southend-on-Sea
Southport
Staffordshire and the Potteries
Stratford and South Warwickshire
Tees
Warwickshire
Wigan
York

OTHER TRUE CRIME BOOKS FROM WHARNCLIFFE

A-Z of London Murders
A-Z of Yorkshire Murders
Black Barnsley
Brighton Crime and Vice 1800-2000
Durham Executions
Essex Murders
Executions & Hangings in Newcastle
  and Morpeth
Norfolk Mayhem and Murder

Norwich Murders
Strangeways Hanged
Unsolved Murders in Victorian &
  Edwardian London
Unsolved Norfolk Murders
Unsolved Yorkshire Murders
Warwickshire's Murderous Women
Yorkshire Hangmen
Yorkshire's Murderous Women

Please contact us via any of the methods below for more information
or a catalogue
WHARNCLIFFE BOOKS
47 Church Street, Barnsley, South Yorkshire, S70 2AS
Tel: 01226 734555 • 734222 • Fax: 01226 734438
email: enquiries@pen-and-sword.co.uk
website: www.wharncliffebooks.co.uk

DNA INVESTIGATIONS

Murder and serious crime
investigations through DNA and modern forensics

Stephen Wade

First Published in Great Britain in 2009 by
Wharncliffe Books
an imprint of
Pen and Sword Books Limited,
47 Church Street, Barnsley,
South Yorkshire. S70 2AS

Copyright © Stephen Wade, 2009

ISBN: 978 1 84563 105 5

The right of Stephen Wade to be identified
as author of this Work has been asserted by him in
accordance with the Copyright, Designs and Patents Act, 1988.

A CIP catalogue record of this book is available from the
British Library.

Printed in the United Kingdom by
the MPG Books Group

Pen & Sword Books Ltd incorporates the imprints of
Pen & Sword Aviation, Pen & Sword Maritime, Pen & Sword Military,
Wharncliffe Local History, Pen & Sword Select, Pen & Sword Military Classics,
Leo Cooper, Remember When, Seaforth Publishing and Frontline Publishing

For a complete list of Pen & Sword titles please contact:
PEN & SWORD BOOKS LIMITED
47 Church Street, Barnsley, South Yorkshire, S70 2AS, England.
E-mail: enquiries@pen-and-sword.co.uk
Website: www.pen-and-sword.co.uk

Contents

Introduction

The wonders of the Victorian age in science and technology took a long time to percolate into forensic science, but after pioneering work by Alphonse Bertillon and by several others across the world, fingerprints were taken into official recognition, and a murder case was solved soon afterwards. By 1900, fingerprinting established forensic work at Scotland Yard as truly based in science. In the 1940s, after two celebrated cases and pioneering work by Sir Bernard Spilsbury, forensic orthodontics was added to the armoury of the forces of criminal investigation. These were attempts to individualise material, investigate more minutely the physical evidence at crime scenes. But behind these significant advances something far more momentous was happening: DNA was being identified and defined in the study of genetics.

There had been blood-grouping of course; work by Karl Landsteiner established the A, B and O blood groups in 1901; and in 1925 it was discovered that blood groups could be ascertained from other body fluids. By the 1960s the Scotland Yard forensic science lab could use bloodstains to relate evidence to suspects with a high level of accuracy. Back in the nineteenth century, blood on a suspect or at a crime scene could not be defined in terms of its origin – it could have been human or animal, and so confusions and uncertainties arose. But DNA (deoxyribonucleic acid) was to revolutionise matters in this area of police and legal procedure.

DNA exists in the sixty trillion cells within the human body. Some DNA is contained in genes, and as genetics has advanced, so has the knowledge of the nature and location of DNA. This is virtually unique in each person, and so the forensic uses are obvious.

Friedrich Miescher first discovered DNA in 1868 but only in 1943 did two scientists, Oswald Avery and Colin McLeod, discover that it held specific genetic information. Then, in 1953, Francis Crick, James Watson and Maurice Wilkins discovered and explained the defining double-helix shaping of the DNA in the cell. It became clear that all humans have a certain amount of the same DNA in common - but not all. From that realisation came a recognition of the practical applications of the knowledge.

Arguably the most celebrated milestone in the history of DNA used in forensics is that of the Colin Pitchfork case (Chapter 3). This followed the discovery by Sir Alec Jeffreys of a method of identifying individuals from DNA. He called the method 'Restriction Fragment Length Polymorphism' which means that sequences of DNA in a shorter length of cellular form could be analysed. Or, in plain English, he called it 'DNA Fingerprinting'. It took until 1987 for the first conviction to be made.

This book aims to tell the story of how the knowledge of DNA led to the revolution in forensics; many of the cases here have been resolved. During the writing of the book, two infamous and controversial cases of savage murder were solved and the real culprits imprisoned for life: Robert Napper for the murder of Rachel Nickell (and others) and Peter Tobin in Scotland also for multiple murders. But other headlines in 2008/09 were equally significant for inclusion.

DNA gives specific information about a person, and can identify a criminal with certainty. As well as meaning that guilty people may be sentenced and imprisoned, it also means that there are very probably innocent people in prison, and that has proved to be the case. Chapter 6 on Lynette White and the 'Cardiff Three' here shows that; and also the very recent and sensational Hodgson case featured in Chapter 22.

But the repercussions of this new knowledge do not end there. In October 2007, the famous case of Dr Crippen, a man hanged for the murder of his wife in 1910, was suddenly questioned.

David Foran and John Trestrail, forensic scientists in America, have stated with confidence that the body in the cellar of Crippen's home at Hilltop Crescent in London was not that of his wife, Cora. Trestrail has said, 'There were no identifying parts of the remains found, no head, no bones, no organs of gender. I've always wondered, who is that under the steps?' But there are some remains of tissue, and so the mitochondrial DNA there has been analysed. This is the DNA from the maternal ovum, passed down from mother to daughter. This kind of DNA is present for longer in remains and is undiluted. A match with the mother is easily made. Foran and Tretrail worked forward in time, tracing relatives of Cora Crippen, and it has been established that there is no mitochondrial link, so the body was not that of Mrs Crippen. Who was she? That is the next question for crime historians and scientists.

Equally significant with this new knowledge was the issue of the uses in terms of a database of DNA for use in future criminal investigation. In December 2008, the European Court of Human Rights in Strasbourg ruled that Britain had no right to keep DNA records of the 857,000 people on the DNA database at that time. BBC News gave the example of teenager Kathryn Lay from Essex who was wrongly suspected of a crime and her DNA taken (as a buccal swab taking saliva) and although she was released, her DNA record was retained. Her mother summed up the issue well: 'I don't have a problem with a database that has everyone's DNA on it... but to collect samples via the back door, and to lump in my daughter with real criminals is not right.'

The magazine for prisoners, *Converse*, proclaimed in its December 2008 issue under the theme of a 'breach of human rights' added, after two Sheffield men had been awarded £36,000 for the infringement of their personal liberties: 'The court found that the police's actions were in violation of Article 8 - the right of respect for private and family life - of the European Convention of Human Rights. It also said it was struck by the blanket and indiscriminate nature of the power of retention in England and Wales.' However, as my case in Chapter 16 shows, the power of DNA in cases where there has previously been a charge and then a more serious offence follows, is immense and the greatest forensic resource available.

Only six months before the decision from Strasbourg, a senior police officer had called for a mandatory criminal DNA register. There had just been two convictions brought about by DNA work: Mark Dixie, and the 'Ipswich Strangler', Steve Wright. DS Stuart Cundy told a TV channel, 'DNA was central to this investigation [Dixie's arrest]. If there had been a national register with all its appropriate safeguards, then rather than nine months before Mark Dixie was identified, he could have been identified much sooner.' But a caveat here is surely to recall that in 2007, a civil servant lost two discs in the post containing 25 million private records of the recipients of child benefit payments.

On the positive side, in November 2007, Maninder Kohli was imprisoned after being found guilty of rape and abduction of a seventeen-year-old girl. DNA matching that of his victim was found in his van. Peter Tobin (Chapter 17) was convicted in 2008 of the murder of Vicky Hamilton many years before, and hope is now evident in many unsolved cases, such as the earliest one in the following chapters, that of Muriel Drinkwater in 1946.

In 1995, the world's first national criminal intelligence DNA database was formed by the Forensic Science Service, and in 2006 the Service created 'DNA Boost' which can separate mixed or 'smudged' DNA from different individuals. In May 2004, the DNA squad focused on 2,000 murder cases and one report noted that, 'At least a dozen unsolved murders in Scotland could be cleared up as a result of the same DNA that linked Angus Sinclair to the World's End killings.' But markedly, that has not proved to be a smooth passage in the courts. Offences have to be recorded on the Police National Computer and this is integrated into a criminal record; the samples may be from blood, semen or saliva.

There is no doubt that the National Database (NDNAD) provides all kinds of advantages to criminal investigation. The probability of two unrelated individuals having a matching DNA is less than one in one billion. A person's DNA is unique – with only one exception – that of identical twins. In terms of what is recorded, the current situation is that rooted hair and mouth swabs have been labelled 'non-intimate samples'; these may be taken from any person arrested for a recordable offence and detained in a police station, and it is not necessary for the sample to be directly relevant to the crime being investigated.

The result of all this is that we have become accustomed to the kinds of newspaper headlines that intend to shock, stories relating to events of decades previously, such as: 'Beatle Beast. Harrison's gardener gets life for rape.' (The *Sun*, 21 July 2008) in which the story told was of a man who was formerly gardener to George Harrison and who had been jailed for a rape committed twenty-seven years ago. The conclusion of the report is now becoming a familiar wording: 'His DNA was matched by a billion to one chance, Bristol Crown Court heard.'

With the other principal repercussion in mind – miscarriages of justice – it has to be noted that the Criminal Cases Review Commission, at a time when DNA has made it more important than ever to investigate sentences on other types of evidence, is strapped for cash. In October 2008, its funding was cut. The case that highlighted this problem was the exoneration of Barry George for the murder of Jill Dando earlier in that year. George's acquittal was the result of a great deal of time and effort: his lawyer said, 'A case like Barry George needed a lot of resources putting into it and whether they would be able to do that in the future is a great concern.' Equally, we now know that Colin Stagg was wrongly arrested and prosecuted for the Nickell murder, and that he suffered, in the words of Grania Langdon-Down, 'Years of abuse' for that. The government has recently arranged to put a ceiling on compensation in such cases: £500,000 for wrongful imprisonment of under ten years and £1 million for more than ten years - to show a parity in relation to payments made to victims of crime.

The following cases cover notorious as well as obscure cases from the records. Most are tales of success and triumph. The present-day conviction of a killer for a murder of many years previously is a remarkable event, and there must be a large number of guilty people who are not sleeping well at night now, knowing that even more sophisticated methods of defining and using DNA samples are being evolved. But some cases here deal with acquittals also due to DNA evidence. There are also the stories of freedom, as a guilty person is charged and a wrongly-jailed person goes free. The recent Hodgson case already referred to (Chapter 22), is an exceptional one. Yet within these tales there is tragedy, perhaps never so poignant as the instance of Stefan Kiszko, who died in 1992, aged forty-two, just two years after his release from prison. Kiszko was proved innocent of the murder of Lesley Molseed back in 1976. He had served fourteen years for a crime he did not commit. It has to be one of the saddest and most darkly ironical and tragic of all the modern chronicles of murder in Britain.

In one sense, the advent of DNA evidence is another in the long line of specialist forensic knowledge that is present in the trials and appeal courts through criminal history, from the learned professors who specialise in ear-prints to the 'bone doctors' who reassemble skulls of victims murdered decades before the investigation goes 'hot' again. But in another sense, it is a totally different significance, opening up yet more possibilities for the exact exhibition, description and proof of an act; it may provide the full extent of all the implications of the famous statement of the founder of forensic science, Edmond Locard, who says of the criminal:

Wherever he steps, whatever he touches, whatever he leaves, even unconsciously, will serve as a silent witness against him. Not only his fingerprints or his footprints, but his hair, the fibres of his clothes, the glass he breaks... the blood or semen he deposits or collects... all of these bear mute witness against him.

This has been summarised in countless text books as, 'Every contact leaves a trace.' Little did Locard know just how far the implications of that would reach into the most minute physiological and chemical traces.

For help with illustrations I have to thank Vicki Schofield, whose artwork has helped to dramatise some of the key incidents in these records. Also, thanks go to Brian Elliott, my commissioning editor, and to David Stock, Catherine Townsend, Ken Lussey and to staff at the Salt's Mill, Saltaire. For debts to other crime writers, thanks go to Andy Owens for the Mary Gregson case, and to Mike Fielder, whose book, *Killer on the Loose*, gives the best account of the initial Rachel Nickell investigations.

Chapter 1

DNA in Forensics Explained

DNA exists in a number of our human cells: in the form of genes, it forms the basis of heredity; in form, the genes are arranged in a chromosome, and these are paired, with twenty-three pairs, two of these being the sex chromosomes X and Y (XY in males and XX in females). The DNA is formed in a string of molecules called nitrogenous bases, and there are four such bases that make DNA: Guanine, Cytosine, Thymine and Adenine. As these became more explored and understood, and the nature of DNA described, it was realised that just these four bases exist in the creation of life, and they are arranged along a strand, and referred to by their initials: CTAG.

The DNA helix shape, discovered by Crick and others, is double stranded, and the bases only connect in the pairings of C with G and A with T. In one cell there will be a certain arrangement of these, in the helix shape, and all these together make the genome. When a scientist looks at a profile of the DNA within a cell there will be a string of combinations of pairings, so the strand might have something like this, with two rows of the sets of pairing: one row could be TACGATGC and so on; the other might be ATGCTACG and so on.

In an individual's DNA there will be three billion of these pairings. The notion of 'fingerprinting' with that degree of individuation of the cell's DNA elements make it clear just how specific a test can be when a match between two sources is attempted. But there is even more of a reduction in the actual nature or quantity of the DNA that is used in forensics. This is because there are two versions of DNA: genes and non-encoded. The latter, called junk DNA, is the source of the evidence in forensics. Logically, the DNA in genes per se is clearly functional and part of a larger, complex unity of cells across the living being. But the junk DNA will exist in all kinds of places within the entity.

The double helix, shaped like a twisted ladder (see the first illustration in the plates) has the pairings of A and T and C and G across itself, so the binding is lateral. The sheer astronomical number of cells and of DNA stored can be understood by considering the pairs of chromosomes from mothers and fathers: one chromosome from the mother to each egg made is separate from the others. One egg will have a vast number of combinations of bases, working out at two multiplied by itself twenty-three times. The result is over eight million types of ova. This is then doubled as the same is applied to spermatozoa. Scientists reckon that the resulting possibilities of different DNA in cells is around eight trillion.

We have to ask, what chance has a suspect in the face of this? If a rapist leaves semen at the scene of crime and then the DNA from that is taken and matched to a database, the evidence that he was the rapist is very hard to oppose in a court of law. DNA can be extracted from blood, sweat, semen, saliva, hair and even tears.

Alec Jeffreys in 1984 showed that DNA is polymorphic: that is, sequences of the base pairing of the four bases are repeated in patterns along the section taken from a location. The sequences that repeat are called satellites, and the patterns of repeated strings and pairings are called variable number tandem repeats. In the first years of the application of DNA to forensics, this was the method used, in abbreviation, VNTR. In contrast to this, another type of satellite sequence was identified, patterns that had frequent repeats through a string, and these have become known as STRs – short tandem repeats. The fingerprinting which was first done, when DNA was just being properly understood, was called RFLP – restricted fragment length polymorphism (RFLP). This required a substantial sample for study and it had to be fresh or preserved well. But today, PCR is the method used – polymerase chain reaction (PCR). This uses short repeats and a method of taking out bits of samples at different places along the strand is used to define an established pattern more quickly.

All this is best understood with the help of an image. The process is like watching a factory production belt move along, with a set of objects in each section all designed to go together. Every so often the collection of items will come along, all ready for packing. Then there will be other sequences in between. In the equivalent in DNA, the scientist sees and samples items along the strand to define the individuality of the DNA.

This is a summary of the methods:

RFLP

This is still used, but requires the extraction from a good source, then separation and transfer to that sequences may be tagged and then matched according to a pattern. What results from this process is a DNA fingerprint looking rather like a swatch strip showing colours on a band. This is actually a set of bands visualising the DNA pattern using sheets of x-ray film. The resulting strip is an autorad. The line of bands of varying thickness can then be compared to the other sample to look for a match. These patterns of markings are in columns called lanes. Any similarity between the two samples from different locations would be soon identified if they matched.

Polymerase Chain Reaction (PCR)

PCR was used first in 1992, and this shows the repeated strings in a DNA pattern. Amazingly, this needs only a billionth of a gram of DNA material to be studied. The double-stranded patterns in the AT/CG couplings will be in certain permutations, so that in one sample of semen for instance, there could be a sequence with ATGCGCTT and that would be logged and matched. In addition, by denaturing, the two strands can be separated so that they can be seen separately, and this is done by heating to 96 degrees F. Even more impressive is the discovery that the process may be speeded up by 'annealing' – bringing out the sequence patterns in a way similar to using predictive texting on a mobile phone.

Short Tandem Repeats (STR)

STR arrived in 1994 and this involves looking at tiny microsatellites in the cell that repeat. The huge advantage here is that this may be used on poor quality samples where some material may have been degraded. Together with PCR, the STR provides a formidable evidential product for the lawyers and police. The combination means that results may be obtained in just a few days. Fragments taken can be separated by a gel electrophoresis, linked to a computer so that a printout can be taken. Another way of presenting the DNA profile is as a graph, similar to that showing heart rate at the end of the hospital bed, or the graph that shows speech utterances in phonetics.

Single Nucleotide Polymorphism

This is the attempt to use just one nuclear base in the study. It involves a search for a designated sequence, much like a security number used in internet banking, where, say, every sixth base is G and every third is T and so on. The search then looks for these sequences. The question then arises about what would be the odds that another person somewhere on earth would have the same sequence and pattern of DNA material? The fact is that such a match to another person would happen in the trillions – as in a sequence of places where a pattern occurs at these numbers in the sequence: 6-9-8-4-3-5-6-2 paired with another eight numbers; the fact is that the inheritance of the DNA patterns at one place in the chain is different from any other place, the possibilities of a match with another person is, as Dr DP Lyle has stated: '12 out of ten billion' unless identical twins, where the DNA is identical.

In more recent cases, the advances have been with dealing with degraded DNA material. This is all about individualising the DNA, and by the side of what used to happen at the beginning of the professional police force, the difference is astronomical. In the 1829 issue of the *Police Gazette*, for instance, this was the only real method available in attempts to locate a criminal:

Frauds and Aggravated Misdemeanours

A man, about seventy years of age, five feet six or seven inches high,

Stout made, hair powdered, full faced, blue undercoat, and wore a dark

Shabby greatcoat and white neckcloth, had a respectable appearance,

And speaks several languages, carries a black stick and a small square

Parcel in oil cloth, and said his name was Lewis… obtained on false Pretences… two gold watches, one of which was stamped 'A.S.'…

The above accounts of the various methods of identifying an individual would have seemed like the most bizarre science fiction to Victorian police. Today, even degraded DNA such as material damaged by heat or decay may be used. SNP analysis will arguably become the norm, as it is most effective in this application as well as in the more mainline tasks.

The final aspect needing explanation is the subject of where DNA is found. Virtually any cellular material left at the scene of a crime may be analysed. Blood, saliva and semen are the most widely used and discussed in press reports, but there are others, and some of these sources mean that different types of DNA are studied. In blood, only white blood cells have DNA, but of course, this presents no problem. It simply means that the white cells have to be separated out from the rest of the sample using a technique where the sample is spun at different speeds to separate out parts of different densities. The red have no nucleus, and so no DNA.

With semen, what happens is that the semen has travelled down the urethra and along the lining of that duct there are cells called epithelial cells, and these have DNA in them. Naturally, some of these cells collect in the semen and so the semen is then usable in analysis. Of course, there is one important point to be made here: this is that in the case of a man who has had a vasectomy operation, because clearly that individual will not have produced sperm, so there would be no DNA, as there has been no sperm moving, that would collect the cells in the urethra.

Again, it is epithelial cells that give the source of the DNA in saliva and in tears. A buccal swab (taken in the mouth) is the most commonly used method of taking cellular material from a suspect. Of course, the advantage here is obvious: saliva and liquid in the tear ducts are acting like a preservative, and the cells there are retained in a tight, easily accessible space, so the sample is very easily taken.

Hair is a rather different proposition. This is because there is no typical junk DNA in the hair strand itself; the DNA is in the follicle at the base of the hair, the root base of growth. Therefore, only hair that has been ripped out by force will have accessible DNA. Naturally, a chunk of hair with follicles, taken from a scalp, will present the analyst with cellular DNA in the materials around the follicles also.

As will be seen in the next chapter on Oetzi, the mummified corpse found in the Alps, DNA in bones is present but is of a different type: this is in cells called osteocytes, and the material there may be accessed many centuries after the death of the entity in question. Teeth, being the most durable constituents of a corpse, provide very useful DNA material. This is due to the long-lasting pulp cells beneath the enamel. Accessing these cells through the enamel can give access to the DNA in the pulp cells, and that can be done many centuries after the death of the individual.

As mentioned in the introduction, with regard to the investigation of the corpse in Dr Crippen's cellar, mitochondrial DNA has its place in this forensic science also; in the mitochondria, the material around the egg, there are tiny molecules within the cells called organelles, and these have mitochondrial DNA. This is passed maternally and can be located in parts of the body which may not have other junk DNA material. As one medical textbook expresses it:

> *Since mtDNA only undergoes a significant mutation approximately once every 6,500 years it is unchanged over many generations. This means that your mtDNA is virtually identical to your mother's, your great-great-grandmother's and your maternal ancestors' from one thousand years ago.*
> D P Lyle (see Bibliography).

The most famous murder case involving the use of mitochondrial DNA is surely that of the Boston Strangler. When one of his victims' body was exhumed and studied in 2000, semen was found; the source contained mtDNA and the aim was to try to prove that Albert de Salvo, a man assumed to have been the Boston Strangler, was her killer. But he was long dead, so his brother was used as a source of a sample to see if the mtDNA in the body matched his. If it did, then his would be the same as his brother's and so de Salvo would have been confirmed as the killer. But the samples did not match. The Boston Strangler mystery continues as a result of this: not the issue of whether or not specific victims were de Salvo's victims, but whether he was the killer labelled as 'The Boston Strangler' as in both the court process and in the press reports at the time.

As most of the following case studies show, the process of moving from the acquisition of DNA at crime scenes or from individuals in the course of an inquiry is one thing: the use of this in a court of law has been quite another. This stunningly revolutionary new science has had a rough road into the criminal justice system, but the future looks much less bright for offenders, whose DNA will be littered across their trajectory of crime. No more is the standard television image of the villain washing 'clean' the place of a murder something that can be viewed with a sense of outwitting detection. The hoover and the detergents for the floor, together with the white gloves, are no longer enough to give the criminal a sense of security. The dictum that 'every contact leaves a trace' has now gone from what may be found in the grass or in the cracks of concrete to what has been present in a human body in absolutely minute, microcellular condition.

Chapter 2

From Oetzi to the Garda's National Bureau

On 19 September 1991, the body of a man was found in the Oetzal Alps by two hikers. The figure was lying face down, and in ice. This was a victim of a murder, but one that happened around 3,000 BC. The hikers told the authorities and soon there were scientists on the scene as well as police. The ice had been melting in that valley for a while and, just a few weeks before, two other bodies had been found nearby, but these were two climbers who had died in 1934.

Despite the death being so long before, the finders had still been reckless, not particularly thinking about the work of archaeologists; one man drilled into ice and cut into the iceman's bone. But eventually the body was in a coffin and taken away for analysis. Pictures were taken and then questions were asked about the corpse that was to be named Oetzi. Pollen and dust were analysed; study of his teeth revealed that he had been born near Bolzano but had gone to live in the higher valleys.

It was a murder case and DNA information was to provide the basis for a narrative of Oetzi's life and violent death. There were some obvious features which gave some immediate clues, such as the tattoos on his limbs that suggested some kind of acupuncture treatment, and there was evidence of some damage done to him by a parasite called whipworm. But soon the DNA work gave some results. The mtDNA showed that he was part of a rare group, known in the Alpine region studies as K1. In other words, he was from that area and his people always had been so. He was in his fifties when he died and that means that he was unusually healthy and robust, in spite of the whipworm. His stomach showed that he had eaten a meal not long before death and his clothes were easily imagined from residual traces and fragments. He carried an axe and a flint knife. But he had definitely been in the wars.

Oetzi was holding a knife when he died and he had been shot by an arrow, which caused his death. The shaft had been broken off, and sophisticated x-ray scans showed that he had a deep arterial wound under the collar bone. He had died of a cardiac arrest after blood loss. All this shows a pattern of study involving DNA as well as other methods of analysis, and even in a case from so long ago, there are incredibly minute details of his life and death evident here. The DNA study played a part in this, and we know that he was almost certainly killed.

If all this can be achieved from a 4,000-year-old killing, what can be done regarding murders in the last fifty years or so? In addition to the databases, there are now special units and departments in the police forces of the UK dedicated to this work. In Ireland, for instance, the Garda Cold Case Unit was established in 2008 to work on a number of unsolved murders. The case of Brian McGrath shows the success of this initiative. The news broke in January 2009 that there had been a significant development in the McGrath case: a file has been sent to the DPP with charges made against suspects.

Brian had been killed in March 1987. The father of four handyman was beaten to death and then buried near to his home at Coole, near Castlepollard, County Westmeath.

After his disappearance, it was assumed that he had gone to find work in Holland, but now that is known to be untrue and the body has been located. Brian McGrath was brought up at the Artane Boys Industrial School and then served in the army, leaving with an honourable discharge, then he married in 1977. At first they lived in London but then went home to Ireland, and the family man was happy living at Coole. He got by doing casual work, and reports say that he was always a helpful man and a good neighbour. Clearly, his disappearance would be a puzzle, and there was a large-scale Garda investigation. Eventually, in 1993, there was a confession by someone involved in the murder.

After that confession, digging began and the body was found. The woman also named another person involved and today the Garda have the two suspects under investigation. *The Tribune* reported in December 2008 that 'McGrath's widow Vera now lives in Navan, County Meath, with her grandson, Leon. The murder sent shockwaves through the small community in Westmeath... Mystery has surrounded his death...' But now the Cold Case Unit has moved in and evidence is being located. The *Irish Independent* has reported that, after a confession, 'The suspect made a number of key admissions when questioned by detectives in 1993... an examination of remains exhumed on Monday morning was continuing yesterday at the Dublin City Morgue in Marino.'

The McGrath case is one of 200 being studied by the Garda Cold Case Unit; they are based at the National Bureau of Crime Investigation in Harcourt Square, Dublin, led by Superintendent Christy Mangan. The team working there, according to the *Irish Independent's* report on 4 January 2009, consists of a forensic anthropologist, DNA analyst and other specialists.

The link with Oetzi is evident, as the writer of the *Independent* article made clear: 'Forensic pathology examinations of bog bodies thousands of years old have revealed a wealth of detail about bodies taken from bogs in Ireland, including how they died.' The DNA team will be part of this very efficient unit, the successor of the unit set up by Assistant Commissioner Tony Hickey before he retired in 1998 – a five-police force group which had had a quick success in solving the murder of Phyllis Murphy in Kildare in 1979.

Phyllis Murphy was abducted, raped and murdered just before Christmas 1979. Her body was found a month later at Ballinagee Bridge, near Turloch Hill power station at the Wicklow Gap; some of her clothing was found twenty-eight miles away. At the time, despite a large-scale inquiry involving over 2,000 interviews and a list of suspects, blood tests were used and the man who turned out to be her killer, John Crerar, was eliminated. Phyllis was known as a shy, quiet young woman, not the type to run the kind of risk associated when a lift from a stranger is accepted. But she was last seen at a bus stop. She had worked as a cutter in knitwear factories around Naas and Newbridge.

But then the Cold Case Unit set to work and by gel electrophoresis (Short Tandem Repeats) in the hands of Dr Maureen Smyth and Dr Louise McKenna found a link to Crerar, as his blood taken at the time matched the sample. Officers of Operation Trace arrested Crerar in Kildare. He was in the inquiry net within just ten days, and the last twelve hours of that were spent being questioned at Naas Garda station, where he was charged.

The Garda Cold Cases Unit exemplifies the future of policing with DNA fingerprinting at the centre of forensic back-up. In the case of the Garda's unit, Tony Hickey has to take credit for the thinking behind this. He was the man who hand-picked a team of officers to work on the murder of journalist Veronica Guerin; Hickey, from Kerry, joined the Garda in 1965, and was at first based in Cork but then moved to Castlebar, County Mayo, rising to Superintendent in 1986. By 1996 he was Assistant Commissioner, and he took on the Gilligan gang in the Guerin case. Clearly, his establishment of the Cold Cases Unit was a recognition that, if regional forces worked together and linked with international forensic resources and expertise, such investigations as murders and disappearances with suspicious elements would be tackled in a streamlined and professional manner.

This thinking and the organisation that goes with it, shows the template of how police work goes hand in hand with forensics. In the murder of Phyllis Murphy, for instance, the Dublin tests were reported to the London base for checking, and although the DNA extraction procedures are standard and unified, the communication and support from further afield is essential of course.

The Irish organisation also provides the interesting link between forensic science and archaeology: the knowledge of the bodies in the bogs (prominently displayed at the National Museum of Ireland in Dublin) clearly provided a foundation of relevant knowledge in the McGrath case and will prove to be useful again. In much the same way as 'bone doctors' have to try to reassemble skeletal remains from excavations, the work of the DNA scientist is similarly revivifying 'dead' material – it is a very impressive revisiting of long-dead material which has within it, nevertheless, minute sources of evidence which may condemn a criminal when other approaches have failed. The killers of Brian McGrath must have thought that they were untouchable, and John Crerar may have slept easily for many years, but retribution came, and in the shape of science, with its accomplice, the police specialist.

South Yorkshire Police also have a very busy and successful Cold Case team. Superintendent Richard Fewkes reported to the South Yorkshire Police Authority in December 2007 that a mixed team of civilian specialists and police officers had reviewed fifty cold cases and there were at that time another fifty investigations in progress. He commented that South Yorkshire had a good system of preserving crime scene materials for future use in DNA work. Many of the cold cases were, as in the case almost everywhere, offenders of 'stranger rape'.

Chapter 3

The Historic Cases:
Colin Pitchfork and Robert Melias
1983–1988

On 29 January 1987, a forty-three-year-old woman, disabled with polio, had an intruder in her home at Avonmouth. The person who had broken in was Robert Melias who raped his victim. A forensic scientist who later worked on high-profile cases with DNA, began his work in that field in 1979 and commented in an interview in 2009 that 'In 1979, the police had never considered using DNA science as part of an investigation.'

But on the Melias case, and on 13 November 1987, Melias pleaded guilty to rape and was given a sentence of eight years behind bars. It has been the first prosecution that had used DNA fingerprinting in the UK. Bristol Crown Court suddenly became a location of great significance in the history of criminal justice. The man who headed the team involved was DC Clive Tippets, and he commented recently at the twenty-year anniversary of that event: 'At the time I realised that it was a great scientific breakthrough, but did not foresee the advances in its use. Today, the smallest samples from historical cases can lead to identifying the offender...'

The name of Melias is hardly a household word, but the name of Colin Pitchfork will always be associated with the advancement of DNA. Just over a year after Melias was convicted, Colin Pitchfork was sentenced to life imprisonment by Mr Justice Otton. January 1988 became the next great milestone – the first conviction for murder by means of DNA sampling. The basic facts of the Pitchfork case are simple but there is much more. His first victim was Lynda Mann, who went missing in November 1983 near Leicester; her body was found and she had been raped and strangled. The first investigations took place near the Carlton Hayes hospital – a place where sex offenders were placed – but enquiries came to a dead end. In July 1986, Dawn Ashford's body was found in the same area, and she had been raped and strangled. A young porter actually confessed to the murder, but his statements did not match the known facts. DNA matching was then applied and he was cleared. On the spot at the University of Leicester was Dr Alec Jeffreys, and his new fingerprinting method was applied, and after a ruse in which Pitchfork persuaded someone to give a sample in place of him, nevertheless, Pitchfork was eventually found and charged.

We know a great deal about this case because forensic profiler Paul Britton was involved in the case and in his book, *The Jigsaw Man* (1997) he gives extensive details. Of course, Alec Jeffreys' work is central to this; in September, 1984 he had completed an experiment to find out if repeated sections of DNA could be used to track inherited diseases through families. He said in an interview in 2000: 'The last thing I was thinking about was paternity suits or forensics. But I would have had to have been a complete idiot not to spot the implications.' The rapes of Mann and Ashford around Narborough meant that he was invited to test the man who first confessed. The police asked Jeffreys to prove that the man, Richard Buckland, had murdered Lynda Mann. At first, the tests showed that the two women had been raped by the same man but that Buckland was not the man. The findings were not accepted by the police who told him that his technique was 'a dud'. But there was much more to come.

The police began the mass sampling of local men, taking blood and giving this to Jeffreys to analyse. There were 4,000 samples but Pitchfork had avoided taking the test and so his sample was not taken and no match was found at first; but he was soon found out and investigated.

Paul Britton was there to log the police investigation. He was a clinical psychologist at the time, working for Leicestershire Health Authority and was sometimes based at Carlton Hayes. While the more biologically-centred work was going on, Britton was thinking like a profiler: '... I knew that her killer was more than a caricature or comic-book villain. He also had a rich life which had shaped his personality and actions. What went through his mind, I wondered, when he saw Lynda? What did he see and why did he choose her?'

But then, on 2 January 1987, the *Leicester Mercury* carried the headline, 'Blood Tests for 2,000 in Killer Hunt'. We have to recall that this was right at the very beginning of the arrival of DNA in England as a forensic tool. There was mystery and perplexity around the area. Paul Britton recalls that it was referred to at the time as 'The Bloodings' by the press.

As for Pitchfork, he was a baker, aged twenty-five, who had moved to Leicester not long after the Mann murder. When interviewed later he said that he had taken his wife to an evening class and then picked her up again later in the evening, on the day of the second murder. The couple had a baby and he was nursing the child, so that hardly fits with the profile of a serial killer or at least it was a major factor in the thinking at the time. As with the comments on the Yorkshire Ripper investigations, done with hindsight, it has to be said that at this time computers were not widely used by police. In fact, Pitchfork, in trouble before this on matters sexual (he was essentially a 'flasher' in his early phase) had been logged on three different lists: he had been referred by magistrates to

Carlton Hayes after a conviction for indecent exposure.

Pitchfork outwardly must have seemed so ordinary: working initially at Hampshire Bakery in Leicester, then married young; he had been a volunteer worker for Dr Barnado's and become merely a suburban nine-to-five worker, as far as neighbours would be able to assess him. But his undercover life as rapist and killer was soon to become public. When the 'Bloodings' progressed, a man with his passport was tested and eliminated from the inquiry, but that man, Ian Kelly, loosened his tongue in a pub in Leicester while drinking with some friends, and he confessed what he had done. He said that Pitchfork had spun him a line and made it seem convincing that he had good reasons for avoiding the blood test. But one of Kelly's listeners went to the police, and Kelly was arrested.

Kelly was charged with perverting the course of justice and the police wasted no time in going to visit Pitchfork at his home in Littlethorpe. He told the stories of the two killings and we now know the events leading to those repugnant rapes and murders. He is reported as giving his confession without remorse, and in a cold and detached manner. When he had gone looking for girls to 'flash' that night he met Lynda, the baby was left in the car. He had met his victim and flashed, then she did something not at all typical of the usual reaction to such shocks: she ran into a dark place along the path. Pitchfork was clearly excited by this, so much so that he went to her and attacked. He raped her and claimed that he strangled her while she was penetrated.

In the case of Dawn Ashworth, he had seen her walk into a quiet lane off King Edward Avenue while he was on his motorbike, and he had stopped and gone after her. This time he moved in swiftly and raped her in a field. Dawn then reacted in one of the ways that one has to respect for sheer courage and survival attempt – she said that she would tell no one and asked to leave. But the killer strangled her from behind. He had raped and killed two fifteen-year-old schoolgirls, showing violence and, in the case of the latter victim, she was more than likely also buggered. The attacks were premeditated and no mercy was shown to the victims. When it came to Pitchfork's application for a term of sentence, in August 2008, heard at the Central Criminal Court by Mr Justice Grigson, these salient facts of his crimes were crucially important in the reconsideration of the situation.

In 1994 he was sentenced to thirty years, which meant that he could be released on parole in 2017, but at the 2008 hearing, as is reported in the court proceedings, 'He should only be released when the Authorities are satisfied that he is no longer a danger to women. In any event, in view of the seriousness, callous and cunning conduct the actual length should not be less than twenty years.' In 1988, when he was sentenced, a judge was not obliged to set a minimum term. Mr Justice Otten at that time did not do so because of the heinousness of the crime, and so there was potential for a revision.

The 2008 court had an option to increase the minimum term and did so: the judge said, 'I fix the minimum term at thirty years on each count of murder, less the four months and a day the applicant spent in custody on remand.'

DNA, after Dr Jeffreys' amazing discovery and research, had caught its first killer in Britain. The gates were open for so much more, and the repercussions were astounding. Semen from both victims had correlated with Pitchfork's – a type A blood group. From there, DNA was introduced and there was no further doubt about the identity of the killer. His killing ground had been known locally as 'The Black Pad' and so he has acquired that tag, 'The Black Pad Killer'. But his dubious notoriety will always be effaced by the revolutionary forensics behind his arrest and conviction. Genetic fingerprinting had moved from a stunningly innovative concept that could potentially bounce forensic science into the headlines for years to come, to something that was actually only the beginning of the process of individuation in crime investigation. We now know, after Melias and Pitchfork, that the latter was the case.

Chapter 4

The Keith Lyon Case
1967–2006

There would be a strong argument to say that not only is the Happy Valley near Brighton wrongly named, but that there is a hex on the place – at least in parts. The village at the heart of this, Woodingdean, is close to the road where, in the annus horribilis of 1967, first Errol Flynn's mother was killed in her Isetta bubble car, and then young Keith Lyon was murdered. The former met her end in a crash on the highest main road in the area, and the latter by a bridle path.

Keith was just twelve years old when, on a Saturday afternoon in May that year, he set off to walk into this scenic area to buy a geometry set. He never came home. He was killed in what was described at the time by DS Roy Yorke of Scotland Yard as 'a frenzied, vicious attack'. *The Times* reported that there had been a suspicious sighting near the murder scene: 'Murder Squad detectives investigating the stabbing… tonight issued the description of a woman, aged between forty-five and fifty-five, they wish to interview. She was dressed in a long grey or green raincoat and had straight, mouse-coloured hair.' Although several witnesses said that they saw this woman around that place, the lead came to nothing.

A massive police hunt followed, and the boy's photo was widely distributed. One feature of the search was that a dummy dressed in clothes similar to those worn by Keith was placed near the murder spot. Over 80,000 homes were visited and questions asked. Police interviewed 2,000 children at seventeen schools. Then when locals were questioned it emerged that there was an established enmity between boys from two local schools, the children like Keith from the 'posh' school often being abused and sometimes assaulted by the pupils from the other school. As Keith went towards the village store for his geometry set, it was suggested he met some teenagers from the rival school; there was allegedly a fight and, as Martin Wainwright in the *Guardian* wrote in 2006, 'In a brief attack, he was stabbed eleven times in the stomach with a serrated kitchen carving knife after a mob of teenagers jumped him, according to local people, they then left him to bleed to death on the path.'

It was a sad and nasty tale. Keith, a bright boy, had been given some money by his father to buy the geometry set, and his father, Ken Lyon, who was a well-known bandleader in Brighton, and was due to conduct a concert at the Metropole Hotel, made a public appeal. Ken had given the boy his pocket money after he had spoken his last words: 'I am going for a walk. I want to buy something for my geometry set.' His father talked about his 'wonderful boy'. Keith had been wearing his uniform for the Brighton and Hove Grammar School.

The first significant development occurred when a knife was found. There had been a report that someone had been seen in a nearby public house trying to wash blood off their clothes and hands. The killer had thrown this steak knife into the bushes, and it must have seemed as though there was a chance that a suspect would be traced. But the trail went cold. Time passed, and Mr Lyon died in 1991. Keith's mother died in 2006, so neither was destined to have any closure in this terrible story. Mrs Lyon had told the press that the affair had ruined their lives.

There had been a development in 2002, however, when workmen stumbled upon a locked storeroom in Brighton police station and found some evidence, including the murder weapon, which was said at the time to have been misplaced. It was later stated, though, that the knife had never been lost, but simply left in long-forgotten storage. In the 1970s, the materials had been bagged and boxed: there was a cigarette and bloodstained tissue. In 2006, there was what seemed to be a breakthrough. There had always been a local tale that a family had emigrated to Canada just after the murder, and with undue haste.

So, in 2006, there was DNA to apply to the materials left in store. At the time of the new developments, a reporter asked a forensic scientist about the tests being done. Jonathan Smith replied, 'It is dust... we can work with cells that have been ignored for years, not least because they are invisible to the naked eye. As long as they have not been got at by the damp or mould, they could still be used even after all this time.'

The BBC programme *Timewatch* had already broadcast a feature on the Lyon case, in 2000 and in 2001, and was to do so again after the announcement of the DNA testing. The knife had been sent to the Forensic Science Service in Lambeth Road. A journalist writing at the time said that security there was tight: 'The lift to the laboratory is crowded with police officers in body armour escorting bags of evidence.'

The account of the DNA work given in *The Independent* at the time raises the level of drama: 'The scientists work behind a closed door that bears a sign saying "Alert! DNA Clean Room." They wear white coats, surgical-style caps and masks, dust cuffs and rubber gloves to move around the lab in which lights are bright and the white surfaces spotless. One scientist at a workbench examines a soiled white boot with a stiletto heel, pausing to draw on an electronic notepad...' What they were doing was applying the Short Tandem Repeat process, as they had degraded samples. It led to something that at first looked like a significant step forward and suspects were found.

The papers were full of the story in August 2006, some

jumping the gun by insisting that the case was solved. There
had been the formation of the inter-force review group even
before the DNA tests, 'an elite team of detectives which applies
the latest scientific techniques to evidence from unsolved
killings'. What really hit the headlines was the fact that arrests
were made. DI Tim Nunn told the press that the arrests were
part of 'one of a number of lines of enquiry we are continuing
to pursue...' Two men were arrested, one in Manchester and
one in Brighton. There was also a resumption of detective work
in Canada. Mysteriously, DI Nunn said he was particularly
interested in hearing about a family and their teenager who
would now be in his late-fifties (in Canada).

Keith had a brother, Peter, who was seven years old when
Keith was killed. He told the press that 'I have had to live my
life with not knowing why my brother died for thirty-nine
years, but knowing that the person or persons who murdered
him is living their life without being punished...' There was
also one ironical sidelight to this, as the *Argus* reported in 2001
that DI Bill Warner was interviewed at that time when a reward
of £10,000 was announced for information leading to the
arrest of the killer. He said that he had been one of the children
fingerprinted: 'I had to go to the science class at Dorothy
Stringer with my mates to meet the plain clothes officers.'
Warner made some powerful statements, including the fact
that the police only wanted 'concrete evidence' and no wild
theories.

Unfortunately, the press furore and the wild claims of a
resolution to the case came to nothing. This is one case in
which the DNA testing, however promising at the time, has at
the moment not led to any breakthrough that will lead to
conviction. Although the media would have us believe that
DNA is the magical answer to all unsolved cases, the fact is
that the steady police work still has to be done – along with the
need for some good luck.

The Keith Lyon story may be doomed to be just another of

those local mysteries, recalled by older residents as they walk on the bridle path. It has already begun to dim in the memory and the dead end of the arrests in 2006 may mean that even the presence of DNA reports and descriptions will not solve the murder; but there surely always has to be optimism in these situations, and hope has to be still nurtured. The DNA work is done, and what remains is further persistent investigation.

One line of thought persists: the circumstances of the murder suggest no other person and no other known motive than the gang attack, a small confrontation which may have escalated into a frenzy. We have similar knife crime now among young people. It may be that the original sighting of the woman near the murder scene was a wasteful distraction and it dissipated energy in the pursuit of the killer. We are left with either a senseless attack by children or a random act of slaughter by a person perhaps insane and on the loose in a quiet place. When someone is located and the suspicions harden into tough questions and a police 'feel' for the right line of enquiry, the DNA material will be there, waiting to condemn.

Chapter 5

The World's End Killings
1977–2008

This is a case of solid DNA analysis being frustrated by two essential components of a murder trial: a clear narrative of events and evidence complementary to forensics being solid and definitive. As I write this, controversy still rages in the Scottish criminal legal system because a man had been acquitted of the murders of two young women in 1977, after a judge ruled that there was 'no case to answer'.

The story begins in 1977 when Christine Eadie and Helen Scott went for drinks after work at the *World's End* public house in Edinburgh. They were last seen alive at 11.15 on Saturday 15 October that year outside the pub in the High Street. Their bodies were found the next day, and in different locations: both in quiet parts of East Lothian, Christine on the shore between Longniddry and Aberlady, and Helen in a field off the road near Haddington. They were both just seventeen and had been friends since school. Helen worked in a kilt shop in Prince's Street and Christine, who was not living at home at the time, worked in a surveyor's office. When they did not return home, parents contacted friends and the police and the search for them was on.

There was a worldwide hunt, with leads being followed up even as far away as Australia. The girls had been seen leaving the pub with two men, so there was a basis for investigation from witnesses. Over 20,000 people were interviewed, and the two murders matched a pattern that was evident in homicides in other parts of the country as well: several young women had been abducted, raped and killed, including three murders in Strathclyde between August and December 1977. Features of the deaths were that most had been sexually assaulted, with ankles tied and gags used. There were two further, possibly linked killings: Carole Lannen in 1979 and Elizabeth McCabe in 1980, both in Dundee. After a Crimewatch programme in 2007, Lothian and Borders Police set up a website and in September 2008, it was announced that DNA analysis had found partial matches at the crime scene and on a database.

As far as the Dundee killings are concerned, in 2004 Tayside detectives set up an incident room to work on these two unsolved cases which may well be linked to the Edinburgh killer. Elizabeth McCabe was a nursery nurse, and her body was found in Templeton Woods in 1980 – only 150 yards from the spot where Carole Lannen's body had been found the previous year. Both had been strangled. Police established the HOLMES system – Home Office Large Major Enquiry System – requesting contact from anyone with information. This is a method that charts and logs all kinds of details as they come in. There were clues: in the Lannen case, she had been seen getting into a red estate car the day before her body was found. There was then a search for a red Ford Cortina, and 6,000 drivers were questioned. In a pattern that fits with the Edinburgh killings, Elizabeth McCabe was last seen at a disco in Union Street at half past midnight, when she told friends that she was going home.

Then, in 2008, Angus Sinclair was everywhere in the daily papers as the man who was to stand trial for the *World's End* murders and the initials DNA were everywhere in the media. Sinclair is a convicted sex offender, aged sixty-two, and has been serving a life sentence for sexual offences, including the strangulation of a little girl in 1961. There was a note of optimism as this was announced – a man in court for a famous unsolved double murder. After all, this was a case of two terrible brutal killings: the girls had been tied up and strangled with their own tights. The announcement made in September 2008 was: 'Detectives leading the investigation into Edinburgh's infamous World's End murders have made a crucial DNA breakthrough.' Indeed they had, but that was just the beginning of this incredibly complex and contentious failure to convict.

Pictures issued of Sinclair sum up the nature of the tale in that context: one image shows a young man with a full head of dark hair; the other shows an old man, spectacled, hair thinning and indeed, to use the cliché, seeming like anybody's harmless old grandfather. DNA work went ahead after the successes of the Cardiff case (Chapter 6) and work was being done on 'low copy' DNA extraction (on degraded samples). DI Allan Jones said: 'We currently hold a DNA profile, linked to both girls, of an unknown man whom we believe may have a direct connection to these murders. In the past few months, the national DNA database, which contains over two million genetic profiles of convicted criminals, has been searched against our profile.'

There was a sense that there was going to be a long-awaited closure. Helen Scott's father told the press: 'It's another progression in the inquiry and I just keep hoping that we will get a conclusion one day.' There was also a televised reconstruction. Before the trial of Sinclair it seemed to many that there would be a conviction. But it was not to be, and the trial caused a rift at the very heart of the Scottish bar. What was also highlighted was the place of DNA in the tranche of evidence and, more interestingly, the basic need for a narrative of the events which were the lead-up to the crime itself.

The defence put forward by Sinclair and his counsel was that his brother-in-law, Gordon Hamilton, was the actual offender in the case. In addition to that, the defence statement was that any sex which had taken place on that night was consensual.

Although there was a great deal of delivery and explanation needed, taking ten days, in order to put forward the evidence, the trial judge, Lord Clarke, at the High Court in Edinburgh said, 'I am of the view that the evidence taken at its highest in context of the whole, is neutral as to whether or not he was involved in acting with force and violence against the girls, there having been some evidence of sexual contact between him and the girls in the twelve hours or so before they were killed.' The prosecutor, in Scotland the advocate-depute, had not satisfied the judge on the ability of the evidence to shift that stated position, so there was nothing put before the jury and no case to answer.

Here was a man in the dock, convicted of culpable homicide and jailed for life in 2001, with DNA linking him to the girls, but he put the blame on another man who could not be questioned as he was dead. The DNA evidence stated that semen from Hamilton was present on both girls, and Sinclair's sperm was present on Helen's coat. The prosecution claimed that the killings were the work of both men together, and the forensic expert, Professor John Mason, also stressed the fact that the girls must have taken around seven minutes to die, as they were strangled with ligatures around their necks. Sinclair was charged with four crimes: abduction, rape, murder and robbery, but the counsel for the defence, Mr Prais, insisted that there was no evidence that could be put against Sinclair.

The failure in court related to the lack of any definite evidence that Sinclair had been present when the girls died. As there was doubt as to which of the two men was actually responsible, there was nothing definite in the charge against Sinclair. What happened next was a furore, a row in which blame was attached principally to the advocate-depute, Alan Mackay. The focus of the matter was why Lord Clarke had stated that there was no case to answer. One answer was that the evidence presented was consistent with consensual sex. Although there was DNA from Sinclair taken from underwear, nowhere was there any certainty that the sex was actually a rape. The DNA evidence was labelled 'low probability' and what this really meant was there was no certainty that the DNA traces on tights were at points at which there would have been a knot in the ligature, or anything that would have suggested that the sex was forced.

The top-level lawyers in Edinburgh had to take some flak: the Lord Advocate was Head of the Crown Office, and there has been much discussion about how and why Mackay failed to present all available evidence, and why there was not a fuller consultation with his superior, the Lord Advocate. In the end, Mr Mackay had to take the responsibility for the failure. There was also criticism of Lord Clarke; it was pointed out in one report that his background was in civil, not criminal law; he had been prominent in the damages claim by Lou Macari against Celtic FC, for instance. Mackay was also up against the charismatic Edgar Prais, a man who had hit the headlines with his journey all the way to St Helena to defend a man on a murder charge, and he had also won an acquittal for Mansoor Khan, accused of money laundering to the tune of £850,000 in a VAT fraud.

What evidence was actually presented? There were genetic traces in the ligatures; semen on the lining of Helen's coat came from Sinclair, and the same match was made between DNA found on the fabric of Sinclair's car, a Toyota Hiace caravanette. Mackay argued that because there were no semen stains on the girls' knickers, the deduction was that the knickers had been used as gags, as Helen's knickers were found by her face. All this was supposition of course. DNA made it certain that the traces found in the knots in the tights made a profile for Hamilton that was a complete match and one for Sinclair that was a partial match. A forensic scientist giving evidence said that the evidence from the tights suggested that they had been 'gripped hard' and so the hint was that there had been violence, and so consensual sex was unlikely.

Strangely, the jury heard nothing about the different knots used – which would have suggested two different men involved. The same applies to the valuable information regarding the girls' characters: they were not prostitutes, and in fact Helen was a virgin. There was no question of any sexual promiscuity. These suggestions give some kind of minimal narrative of the events of that awful night in Edinburgh and what must have been a terrifying drive out into isolated country, beyond any hope of help for the victims.

All the supposed 'evidence' was dismissed by Prais. There was nothing to say that Sinclair had been in the *World's End* that night and nothing to make it certain that he had committed a rape. Prais actually took on the scientist who spoke about the DNA evidence that linked Sinclair to the ligatures. After the objection, the jury never saw the forensic report. The basic fact was that no amount of DNA evidence could ascertain that Sinclair had tied up the girls.

Regarding the possible other murders in the West of Scotland, there was no DNA match there. What had happened was that there had been a convincing narrative of the last night of the two girls in the mind of the investigation team, but in a court of law that had not been a watertight account: the fact that Hamilton was dead meant that unanswered questions would stay that way, in spite of all the good scientific work done by the Scottish forensic science service.

The outcome was momentous, in that, as was reported in *The Scotsman* on 15 January 2009, Scots law was in need of review. Kenny MacAskill, the Justice Secretary at Holyrood, announced that there was to be a review of some of the basic tenets of Scottish law. In Scotland, the double jeopardy rule still applies (it was abolished in England in 2005) – that a person cannot be tried a second time for an offence, precluding any use of any further DNA work. Also, there is a ban on information relating to previous offences being stated in court. That too would have been an asset in the Sinclair case.

There is also the dictat holding firm the power of a judge to conclude a trial without going to the jury. The 'no case to answer' decision was entirely in the hands of Mr Justice Clarke. On top of that is the Moorov Doctrine which states that there have to be at least two sources of evidence implicating the accused person. This is based on the need for two statements confirming two instances of similar conduct. To come out of law school, and to put it simply: in the Sinclair case there were no witnesses.

But finally, it has to be said that there was nothing wrong with the DNA analysis in this case. There has been a government review of what testing was done, and the nature of the Low Copy Number test has been described and defended as a useful practice. Professor Brian Caddy, who directed the process of this review, said that it is safe, but could be used 'more effectively'. Low Copy Number, or Low Template DNA has been defended, and the defence is summed up by Professor Alan Jamieson, director of the Forensic Science Institute in Glasgow. He was asked whether in a profile using that sampling, we would know what it meant. His answer was non-committal when he was asked if this should be used in court cases: 'I agree to some extent with the CPS who say it's a case by case basis.'

This technique depends on using very small profiles; it was first highlighted after its use in the aftermath of the Omagh bombings. Professor Caddy recommended that low template testing should be improved but that it is currently 'sound and secure'. There may be statistical anomalies using low copy numbers, and so there would be a shade of doubt in some instances.

Regarding the *World's End* case, it has to be concluded that the failure to convict was nothing to do with the DNA evidence. There is no real blame to be apportioned. The truth may be that legally acceptable evidence – enough to convict the accused – is always multi-layered, and the anomalies in

Scottish law played into the hands of the defence. Arguably, if the trial had been in England, guided by English criminal law, there would have been a very different outcome.

Chapter 6

Lynette White and the Cardiff Three 1988–2003

In his influential book on criminal profiling, *Criminal Shadows*, published in 1995, David Canter writes about his involvement in a murder investigation in Cardiff. He was invited to go to the crime scene - a flat above a betting shop in the red-light Docklands area of the city. He describes the place after the scene of crime officers had been at work there: 'By the time I got there the room had been neutralised in the detailed way that only police scientists and scene of crime officers can do. Every drop of blood, every foreign fibre and hand-dab had been examined, and all that was left were fading brown stains on the worn carpet where the pool of blood had seeped through.'

Then, in January 2002, police announced that they had a genetic profile of the killer of Lynette White, the girl who was viciously attacked and murdered in that flat, after a fight over money. The forensic scientists had taken away a length of skirting board and from that a DNA sample had been matched to a woman and her brother's DNA matched the sample at the scene.

This contrast is surely one of the most influential pointers to the incredibly powerful value of DNA technology. David Canter was there as a psychological profiler. His skill had earlier helped to catch the 'Railway Rapist' in Greater London and he was a valued professional contact of many high-ranking police officers.

He went to Lynette's flat expecting to piece together a range of information, asking questions about why a person would kill in that way: Lynette had been stabbed fifty times; her neck had been hacked and her wrist deeply cut. When Canter first went to the scene, people were only just being questioned, and so his account of the immediate area and of the prostitution business in that time and place gives a valuable profile of the context of that murder.

The case has become paradoxically one of the most celebrated triumphs of DNA work but also a nasty tale of police corruption and miscarriages of justice, because three men spent several years in prison following police corruption. But at the beginning, Canter described the milieu: 'When I was introduced to the working women... I had my preconceptions further challenged. Most of the women drinking there were in their break between "johns" ... they were overweight, middle-aged, lacking any overt sensuality...' Lynette White certainly did not fit with that description. She had her pimp, Stephen Miller, but she was young, only twenty when she was killed, with curly brown hair and blue eyes.

Lynette had obviously either met a complete monster or she had suffered the violent results of an argument when a client had totally lost control. There had even been an attempt to decapitate her during what had clearly been a prolonged frenzy of aggression and fury. It must have come as a particular shock to many who knew her because, as one of her friends said about her: 'She was really a good worker there. She had a lot of nice gentlemen friends, a lot of regulars. A lot of them tried to get her away from Miller.'

Canter and other consulted experts tried to assemble a number of motives and meanings, including the notion that the manner of the killing was a symbolic act, making her into 'a non-person'. But the accounts given by others stress the sordid, vicious nature of the attack. One irony that was not missed was the fact that Lynette had been murdered on St Valentine's Day.

But whatever 'meanings' are in the array of death and disorder at the crime scene, the result in the first phase of this story is that five local men were arrested and tried; at the first trial, the judge died, and so there was a second attempt in June 1990, at which two men were cleared but three men – Stephen Miller, Yusef Abdullahi and Tony Paris – were given life sentences.

Before there was even a hint of any DNA work, a journalist called Satish Sekar investigated the arrest and questioning of the men by police. Sekar found out about a sorry tale of police bullying, intimidation and bias. It became known that Miller's 'confessions' were the result of intimidation. At the Court of Appeal in 1992, tapes were heard which included Miller's confession. The officers shouted at him and behaved abominably, and a lawyer sat in the room through it all. Their trial had been in Swansea, not Cardiff, and Sekar pointed out that in Swansea, black defendants would hardly be observed by jurors whose lives compared in any way to their own.

The conviction of the 'Cardiff Three' was quashed. In the following investigations into the police behaviour, twenty-two people were held; there was an internal inquiry and after the conviction of the real killer, several officers were arrested. But on 4 July, the real killer of Lynette confessed after the DNA evidence was gathered. Jeffrey Gafoor, a security guard working near Bridgend, appeared at Cardiff Crown Court and as the *Daily Telegraph* reported, 'There were gasps from the packed public gallery as Gafoor, wearing a dark blue jumper, pleaded guilty to the murder...' Gafoor was sentenced to life by Mr Justice Royce.

The killer had been traced after a DNA sweep; after the skirting board had been taken from the flat, a DNA profile was found on it. The profile was called 'cellophane man' by scientists because a similar previous sample had been taken on a strip of cellophane. At Lynette's flat in James Street, the DNA had been found on some paint and taken on a strip. Then a search was made of the national DNA database and no match was found.

Another mass screen by South Wales police cancelled out another 300 possibilities. That was certainly a point of frustration, made even more fruitless when the people who were first questioned were also tested and ruled out. But there was hope in that one of the components in the sample was rare. Andrew MacDonald, forensics expert, told the press that only around 1-2% of the population would have this particular component in their 'fingerprint'.

A trawl for that component on the national database brought 600 names. That was then narrowed down to seventy, and there was a main suspect in there. The person they found was not cellophane man but there was such a match that it was going to be a 'family affair' and indeed the close relative of the profile taken from the national database was Jeffrey Gafoor. DC Williams said in 2003, 'I was one of the officers who obtained a mouth swab from Gafoor that was sent to Forensic Alliance who fast-tracked it. Within twenty-four hours we had the full hit on the database.'

Forensic Alliance was created in 1997, in response to a demand for a more concentrated and tightly organised scientific base for DNA testing; it was made by Forensic Access, Britain's main consultancy in the field, which was formed in 1986, at the very beginning of DNA applied to police investigation. The Alliance has a formidable reputation for the use of innovative and ground-breaking forensics. References to the organisation in the recent history of police investigation suggest, as in this case, a remarkable speed as well as accuracy from the experts there. The Alliance is now part of LGC Forensics.

In some aspects of the depressing and shocking chronicle of the miscarriage of justice in this story, we have an example of a real drama and an outrageous injustice almost stealing the headlines from the DNA profiling. The *Western Mail* summed up the stunning nature of that story in 2007 by stating: 'Senior detectives in re-enquiry to be disciplined for making false statements: one promoted to Home Office Policing Standards Division.' In

February that year four people were charged with perverting the course of justice in connection with the Lynette White murder.

Of the five local men arrested in 1988, three were cleared, but the others in 'The Cardiff Five' (cousins John and Ronnie Actie in addition to the 'Three' listed earlier) but it was not until June 1990 that a second trial took place. The 1992 ruling of a gross miscarriage of justice had behind a complex and utterly disgusting back-story which has been given to the world by journalist, Satish Sekar. Sekar now runs the Fitted In Project, a campaign to make known and to combat any miscarriages of justice that come to the attention of writers and researchers in law. In addition to his book, *Fitted In*, he was also involved in the film, *In the Name of the Father*. Since the acquittals of the Cardiff Three and the subsequent arrest and imprisonment of Gafoor, Sekar has maintained a commentary on the events of that now proven police bullying which gained charges and committals.

As recently as January 2009, Sekar has written on the salient events of that miscarriage. The focus of attention is first, the interrogation of Stephen Miller, and second the statements given under duress and threat by people now serving a sentence for perjury. As Sekar points out, legal history was made in 2008 when Mark Grommek became the first person to be held responsible, by a jury, for the part he played in that travesty of 'justice' when the Three were sentenced. Amazingly, the judge and jury had heard tapes of the police interrogations, threats and intimidation and these were truly shocking. For instance, Mr Abdullahi was called an 'evil, wicked man' by detectives, and it had been shown that he had been working on a ship in dock at the time of the killing – MV *Coral Sea* – a long way off in Barry, as Lynette was slain.

In late 2008, Grommek and two others were imprisoned for perjury in this case, and as Sekar points out, in the case of the woman involved, there were threats made to her baby son as well as to herself. He writes: 'These were weak people who cracked under pressure. Vidlay was told that she would be prosecuted and her baby son effectively orphaned. She was shown pictures of young children to emphasise the point. Unlike Grommek and Psaila, her acquiescence was protecting not just her own interests, but that of her infant son, too.' It is important to stress what Sekar has said here on these intimidated people: 'They have no significant convictions subsequently and Vilday became an exemplary mother – a person her children have been sentenced to do without.'

But Grommek also had to suffer threats of prison, done abusively and violently; this had all been part of something more serious in many ways – poor processes and performances within the personnel in the trial events, and again Sekar was acutely aware of all this. He notes that the first judge, even after hearing the interview tape, decided that Miller had not been 'oppressed'. The judge died before he could deliver his summing-up, and Sekar points out that 'Defence lawyers had counted at least forty points for appeal from it alone.'

All this work by Sekar and the detailed reportage of the latest events means that the DNA part in this might be overlooked, but in spite of the legal significance of the ordeal of the innocent people who will always be labelled the 'Cardiff Three' it has to be recalled that forensic science eventually found Gafoor. Although there was a long gap of time between the freeing of the three people in Cardiff and the arrest of the real killer, DNA brought about the closure in this case.

Finally, under all the hype, debate and repugnance for corrupt police staff in this sorry tale we have the original story of a young woman mercilessly cut down and treated with totally inhuman brutality by a man who allowed others to rot in jail when they had committed no offence. It highlights the vulnerability of prostitutes, even when they have a room, a 'minder' and a community of fellow sex workers. Going back to David Canter's thoughts, as a profiler, on this case, we have to recall that the staggeringly high level of violent crime against prostitutes has to tell us something about the need so many of the psychopaths have in urban modernity to wreak hatred and death on another person, to assert in some sick way their strength and power. Canter's thoughts in his book were that, referring to the White killing, 'This is the type of murder carried out by a person who is impulsive and easily loses control, who drifts from one way of surviving to another...' He refers to Nilson and Sutcliffe; a hundred other prominent types of criminals could be mentioned; the point is that, in 2009, profiling is beginning to look like a poor amateur third cousin to the star that is DNA matching.

Regarding the legal elements in the White case, it also has to be asked: will there be a Satish Sekar around taking note when the next miscarriage takes place? It has to be hoped that forensic advances will pre-empt this, but as long as there are serious crimes with complex scenarios, the police will be pushed and goaded to charge and convict. Optimistically, it could be that repeats of the Cardiff Three travesty may be avoided, but unfortunately, not all murders are committed by people whose DNA is on the national database.

Chapter 7

Andrezej Kunowski
1997–2004

This is a story with massive unanswered questions. It is a chronicle of killing and raping by a man dubbed most recently as the 'Beast of Poland'. The twisted mind of this killer will perhaps never be defined and described.

In May 1997, twelve-year-old Katerina Koneva was strangled in her home in Hammersmith. The killer was on the run after raping a young girl in Poland. As Katerina's father came home, worried after a phone call home, he saw a pair of black boots as he looked through the keyhole and he sensed that something was really wrong. Trajce Koneva went inside, after having to batter his way in because the killer had barricaded the door, and came momentarily face to face with his daughter's killer. The man jumped out of a window and Trajce went to chase him. Later, he was to say that the killer, Andrezej Kunowski, was 'so cool... it was so strange. Then I noticed a bit of blood on the side of his face.' Trajce asked him what he was doing in his house. 'He just looked and then ran away.'

The father went in pursuit of the killer, but lost him, as Kunowski threatened a driver with a knife and hijacked a car. When Trajce went home he found the body of his daughter: she was lying with a cord around her neck, part of a Virgin Airways flight bag she had been given as a gift.

This was only the beginning of years of hell for Trajce; he

was not believed when he told the tale of the killer who had escaped. When police came into the house they found Trajce sobbing, bending over his daughter's body; he had cut the cord, and he recalled later that one of the officers asked him to help to try to resuscitate the girl, but he was not able to. He said he was shocked, and didn't want to hurt her. In a few hours he was in a police cell and his wife and son came to see him, certain that he had taken the life of his own daughter. When they arrived, he was wearing a white forensic suit. It is impossible to imagine the depth of the poor man's terror and fear as his own family thought him to be a killer. Later, he recalled how his wife, Zakalina, shouted at him, asking what he had done. She kicked him and screamed at him; his son, Christian, told him he hated him. Trajce said, 'I had lost my little girl – now my wife was attacking me and my six-year-old son was looking up at me with hate in his eyes.'

Following that, when he was released as the investigation went on, the family gradually split apart. He tried on several occasions to take his own life, and this trauma went on until a CCTV tape was accessed, showing Kunowski running away from the home, and then in 2003 he was arrested and charged. But by then it was too late to save Trajce's marriage. The family were Macedonian, trying to start a new life in London, and Trajce was working as a web-designer.

Kunowski, working as a tailor in London, was forty-five when arrested, and behind him was a trail of rapes and killings, reaching back to his first crimes in Poland. In 2004 it was announced that he had been arrested. In the Koneva murder, it transpired that seven witnesses had seen the killer running away, and the video showed Trajce trying to catch his daughter's killer. Kunowski had been tracked down after approaching a Korean student; there had been a nationwide search and appeal for information and the *Crimewatch* programme had featured the Koneva case. After taking the student to his flat, under the pretext of finding her a bedsit, he tied her up, but surprisingly he let her go after she promised to phone him. She went to the police. A DNA sample was taken then, and that matched the DNA on a cardigan belonging to Katerina Koneva. He had also left his fingerprints on the window ledge as he left the Koneva home. The police had their man, and from there it became clear that Kunowski was perhaps implicated in a number of other similar offences.

Kunowski was jailed for life by Judge Peter Beaumont at the Old Bailey in March 2004. Beaumont, the Commons Master Serjeant of London, said to the man before the sentence: 'I have no doubt at all that you committed that offence for the purposes of sexual gratification of some sort.' It had taken a jury of four women and eight men two and a half hours to decide on a guilty verdict.

The police investigations revealed that Kunowski was almost certainly involved in various other unsolved disappearances of young girls. We now know that the man has committed at least twenty-seven serious sexual offences. Detective Chief Inspector David Little said that the killer was 'Probably the most dangerous sex offender I have come across, and certainly the most prolific.' Katerina's mother was more direct and forceful: 'I hope this evil murderer burns in hell.' The sentence was only the beginning as far as the police's knowledge of this extremely dangerous man went: there was a search back to his life in Poland needed before a fuller picture of his criminal trajectory was known. Even today there are gaps in the knowledge.

In Poland he had attacked twenty-five women and children; Polish police said that they had charged the man with the rape of a ten-year-old girl in Warsaw in 1995 but that Kunowski had been released after a general amnesty. His methods were becoming more clearly understood; in Poland, with the earlier crimes, he had tried to choke his victims and tied them up. Most of his crimes had been committed in the town of Mlawa, in north-east Poland where he had worked as a driver for a building firm. Stories of his earlier attacks began to emerge, such as an assault in Warsaw in 1995 when he had burst into a house where he knew he could attack a schoolgirl; he entered, saying he had business with her father, and then told the girl to kiss him. The next move was that he choked her and demanded that she unfastened her trousers. She was almost suffocated and raped, but he did not kill her and she called for help as he was leaving. That led to his capture.

The history of this rapist and killer is one of unbelievable escapes and a certain amount of inefficiency in the law machine. After this crime in Poland, he claimed to have a heart disease and on release for treatment he escaped. That is when he made his way to Britain, and so there was a furore about that emigration at the trial in London. He sold his flat in Poland and came to England with a tourist visa. When his stay extended beyond that date on the visa, he was picked up and it was discovered that he had in his possession some forged documents stating that he was a Portuguese citizen called Jose Marco da Dias.

A closer look at Kunowski's life in Poland and his existence in England helps to show how the trajectory led to the London crimes. He became known as 'The Little Doctor' and was born in 1956 in Warsaw, his name originally being Andrezej Klembert. He was a child of the Iron Curtain, the Warsaw Pact including Poland in that classification. But at two years old he was sent to an orphanage as his entire family were in jail. An interesting sidelight here is that his grandfather was incarcerated in a psychiatric hospital – and for sexual offences. His mother, Elzbieta Klembert, went to live in Mlawa, a small town eighty miles north of Warsaw.

It might not be stretching the imagination and the sense of the power of a place and a culture in the history of serious crime to say that Mlawa has been a troubled place, a town with a dark and tragic history. As recently as 1991 there has been violence there, when locals torched a Romany settlement. But there is also the shadow of the Holocaust over Mlawa: anti-Semitism was rife in the years of the Second World War, and 7,000 Jews from the town died in the camps. One of the most shocking tales from Mlawa is that in 1946 the Jewish cemetery there was excavated and graves were robbed of jewellery and even of gold teeth. Kunowski grew up in the 1960s in the town, with that aftermath of horror and hatred around him.

Of course, it is impossible to make a link between the inner sickness in the future criminal and the social context; far more likely as a route to follow in trying to explain him is the genetic one, bearing in mind his grandfather's deviance and imprisonment. But one thing we do know is that he was a petty thief when a child and also always in fights. He responded to teasing by using his fists, and even as a child he tended to choke his opponents. By the time he reached the age of thirteen, he was placed in a secure unit for juvenile delinquents. But the first serious crime we know about was committed when he was twenty-seven: the rape of a neighbour and then it was known that other charges were against him which led to his first stretch in prison. Between 1973 and the early 1980s, he committed a number of rapes, all with the same pattern of attack and damage done.

The focus of all his assaults and rapes was to strangle, to go for the throat. Paul Britton, in his book, *The Jigsaw Man*, explains the nature of the Kunowski type: 'He periodically experiences a growing urge for sexual control and domination. He needs to express this through aggression, to overpower, dominate, rape and kill a woman. If you look at your records, this man will have come to your [police] attention perhaps for only minor indecency offences.' Such sex offenders may well have a perspective of fantasy with the acts they commit, but as psychiatrists have noted, this fantasy may well be unobservable and may lie deep in the mind of the criminal. Certainly the full story of Kunowski's mental malaise may never be known.

He was released in 1989 after the end of the Communist period in Poland, after serving six years. It is hard to believe that such a man, who had been in jail for over twenty attacks on women and men, could ever re-enter society, and of course he never really did, but he did marry and had a daughter. For a short time he would have seemed normal, working as a salesman. It is surely significant that he was selling cosmetics. What more attractive job would there be for a sexual predator mostly on women than to handle, talk and even apply, cosmetics? But this was not for long; he was still offending and he was jailed again, in Poland. One begins to doubt the effectiveness of the Polish penal system when it has to be noted that not only did the 'Little Doctor' sexually assault cellmates, but he also escaped from prison and duly raped another child. Once again he was arrested and imprisoned and again he escaped.

At last, far too late for the many more victims of this sadistic and perverted killer, a Polish judge realised that a long sentence was essential for him; the man who decided this, Waldemar Smarzewski, stated that 'This was a very important and dangerous case because of the number of victims and what he did to them. I wanted to put him away for longer because he was dangerous. I was sure that if he left prison he would go back to rape and maybe even kill.' He was given a thirty-year sentence, but that was before 1989. So he was freed. In 1992, he raped again – in Mlawa, and in 1995 he slightly changed the pattern and abducted a victim: Agnieska Grybicka, just fourteen, as she walked home from school. It was after his arrest and imprisonment for this that he pleaded the desperate need for an operation, was released for medical attention, and then escaped, starting his plan to come to Britain.

His plan worked out very well: his need for cash was soon

solved because he sold his flat, and then had a false passport made. He travelled through France and then to Dover and finally to London where he arrived by coach in 1996. Of course, he would have been just another one of thousands of Poles coming to Britain for work, all on tourist visas. As he had not been fingerprinted on arrival in Britain, when the Polish police realised where he was likely to be, they issued prints, but there was no set to check here in England, so his new life was begun, a serial rapist and killer loose in London. His pattern of crime seems to be that he would flee to any random destination after a rape, and then steal and take whatever opportunity was offered, so that, for example, after killing little Katerina Koneva he went to the isolation of Herefordshire, existing by theft. One of the most ironical statements made about him was by a farm manager from whom he had stolen in Warwickshire: 'He was a bit of a strange one... he always stuck out in my mind.'

The Little Doctor, even after a brush with the law over his stealing, pleaded hardship when it came to an appeal for asylum. He bolted into obscurity again after playing for time in that way, and although he was turned down, and should have been deported, his whereabouts were unknown.

But in the end, his capture was down to DNA initiatives. Of course, in jail his DNA was known and matched against the database across Europe and the Polish records gave a positive result. DNA had been the provider of the crucial evidence for the trial at the Old Bailey, and again it had been the main determinant of his being charged with the offences back home in Poland. As he started his life sentence in England, police began to look at other unsolved cases that matched his modus operandi. There are several other possible victims. The horrific saga of pain and hatred in the story of the 'Little Doctor' is surely still not concluded; a man with so many crimes on record usually has more that are conceivably yet to emerge and be re-examined. The abiding image of the infinite harm done to others – those who remain alive though they have had loved ones torn away – is that of Katerina Koneva's father, chasing the killer while his daughter lies dead in her own home. The press apportioned blame of course, and all kinds of institutions were criticised during the trial of the monster, including the immigration services, the Polish prison system and indeed the lack of identity-checking processes for visitors with tourist visas. But in the end, the kind of serial rapist in question here is one that is acutely wily, inventive and amoral, all tremendous advantages in a society where anonymity and obscurity are easily provided.

Chapter 8

Appeals Allowed: Three Cases 1994–1997

In the first years in which DNA evidence began to find a place in criminal trials, there were, naturally, teething problems. The Melias and Pitchfork cases had shown what the potential was for catching villains, but gradually the lawyers had to make sure that the expert witnesses and the types of analysis being done could be made to work in a court of law. After all, the complexities of the DNA profiling processes are difficult to grasp. In the early to mid-nineties there were several cases that led to convictions on DNA evidence in the crown courts, but which were found to be unsafe at the Court of Appeal.

The main problem here was that there were different types of sampling being done, and there were also confusions in court over the nature and significance of probability. Various experts tended to argue over these two issues, and confusion arose.

In the mid-1990s, both single-locus and multi-locus tests were being run on semen stains in rape cases, for instance, and these led to disagreements and discussions of possible errors and inaccuracies by experts. The multi-locus probe was the first type used – the RFLP as explained in Chapter 1. It will be recalled that this produces an autorad, a banding, after electrophoresis has been used with a gel to produce this autorad, which can then be photographed to show the pattern of 'lanes'. The single locus superseded this – the PCR as also described in Chapter 1. Here, the focus is on one string and pattern, and uses heating to isolate one pattern.

In several cases at this time in the 1990s, scientists had to explain in court what methods were used and, more importantly, what the chances were that the substances found at the crime scene and the matching done from suspects' bodily fluids would match. People became tied in arithmetical knots over probability. What happened in the early 1990s was that there was a general agreement on the role of the expert in forensics, and with DNA in mind, the important guideline, as stated in a 1997 case at appeal, was 'Whenever such evidence is to be adduced, the Crown should serve upon the Defence details as to how the calculations have been carried out which are sufficient for the Defence to scrutinise the basis of the calculations.' There were other issues, related mainly to court procedure and the role of the judge, but these will become apparent in the following three cases.

Therefore, at this point there is to be a discussion of three cases from 1994-1997 which illustrate these adjustments in the criminal justice system to the new DNA evidence and how it should be used in court. In two of these three cases what was central was what was expressed as 'The Prosecutor's fallacy' and this was put in this way in 1997:

'Only one person in a million will have a DNA profile which matches that of the crime stain. The defendant has a DNA profile which matches the crime stain. Ergo there is a million to one probability that the defendant left the crime stain and is guilty of the crime.'

This means that a barrister has to be very careful in the way he uses the statements of expert witnesses concerning probability.

A recap on the process of DNA testing as it was in c.1995 is helpful here before we look at the three cases. The process begins with the extraction of samples of substances from the crime scene and from the suspect; the DNA is then cut into lengths and sorted – the electrophoresis. What this means is that the samples are put in a gel and then drawn out. The molecules in the sample travel at different rates – the ones with lower molecular rate travel faster. There is then a pattern made and taken in the gel. Then, radioactive DNA probes are applied and an x-ray preserves the band pattern. That is then photographed and so this process, done to both samples, provide two bands to compare.

The issue of uniqueness was there from the beginning in DNA research and sampling. What is then worked out is called the 'random occurrence ratio'. The more the numbers of bands in the patterns are increased, the more distant becomes the possibility that there are other individuals with that DNA profile. It is the arithmetic of those geometrical progressions by various experts that caused chaos in the appeal courts.

A clear example of this is that if one person in a million has a match with the profile sampled, then in Britain, in the case of a man accused of rape, with our current population, the random occurrence ratio of finding another to match is around one in 35 million. The three cases that follow illustrate the two areas of concern at the time as DNA was gradually understood as a foundation for the provision of evidence: the appeals here were a mix of both expert witness testimony weaknesses and errors made by legal professionals as they, too, wrestled with the implications of 'random occurrence ratio'. Courts have always been used to using expert witnesses, of course, in every known field of knowledge and expertise, but DNA was special from the start – it offered the prosecution team something that has statistics relating to the likelihood that the person in the dock was guilty – expressed succinctly and powerfully. If a murderer stood there facing the jury and they were told that there was a one in several million chance that someone else did this killing they were trying to understand, then they would be most impressed.

The first case concerns the preservation of DNA samples. As discussed in the introduction, the recent ruling at the European Court of Human Rights has made this a very contentious issue. In 1995, it proved to be the means of acquittal for a convicted rapist. At that time a DNA profile had been admitted at a second trial and the issue was whether or not this was admissible. The determining legal guidance was in the 1984 Police and Criminal Evidence Act, which stated:

If (a) fingerprints or samples are taken from a person in connection with the investigation of an offence; and (b) he is cleared of that offence, they must be destroyed as soon as is practicable after the conclusion of the proceedings.

The appellant was convicted of a rape committed in 1989. There had been a match in the crime scene stain and in his own from a previous charge of which he had been acquitted. The DNA sample had been used as part of the prosecution four years after the alleged offence. The appeal court ruled that this was an element of unfairness in the trial.

The alleged rape had taken place in October 1989 and the arrest took place in 1993. Both semen and head hair had been taken for sampling and matching. What made it more difficult for the resolution of the scientific material was that two experts disagreed over the probability: one thought it was 80,000 times more likely that the semen at the crime scene came from the appellant than from someone else; another witness insisted that the probability was 1,250-1 for the hair sample.

Matters might have been more clear-cut had there not been a problem with supposed identification of the accused at the first trial. The victim had described three physical features which fitted the accused; but the man served an alibi notice showing he was about a thirteen minute car journey away from the crime scene.

At the trial, before appeal, the judge had rejected a submission for the DNA evidence to be discounted. The background to this was a glitch in the Metropolitan Police DNA database in 1991, as this was suspended pending legal advice and so the accused's DNA profile was not on that database when he was charged with the rape of two women. If it had been logged, there would have been a pointer to a straight match on the computer.

But in the end, the fact was that the DNA was not destroyed as soon as that became possible. It was ruled to be inadmissible at the Court of Appeal.

The second case concerns two rapes for which a man was sentenced to twelve years in prison in 1990. The first rape was of a woman in her ground floor flat, in the early hours of the morning in 1988. She could describe her attacker and said he was a black male, perhaps in his twenties, clean shaven, and with short hair. He was also wearing glasses. The man had forced open a window.

The other rape showed the same pattern, but on this occasion the assailant had a knife and told the victim to shut up. The description given matched the first account very closely. There was also a report by a police constable of a sighting of a man loitering and looking into the ground floor of a building in that area. The man tried to move away but was stopped. There was no weapon found on him, but he was found near to the location of the offence.

Naturally, evidence was given first regarding the blood matches, and the accused was a B secretor, matching that in a vaginal swab from the victim. On top of that, the DNA tests were done, but that was the source of the issue at appeal. There was a fault in the procedure, summed up in the appeal report: 'It was discovered that the results from the control tracks at the side of the gel [electrophoresis was used, as usual] … were not consistent with the known values for the control DNA...' This was made worse for the argument against acquittal when the phrase 'rogue reading' was used. This referred to a temperature variation in the centre track of the gel, and the term used was that this was a 'dip' or a 'smile' in the readings.

There is nothing in court more certain to impress and influence a judge and jury than a process of forensic practice gone wrong. Even if there has been nothing 'wrong' there is still the point that as expressed in court, if there is no fluent and convincing account of what the test has been, and the slightest mention of an error or an anomaly in procedure, then the case is altered for the judicial thinking. Because the figures for probability were the crucially important factors, any suspicions of wrong thinking there would lead to important conclusions.

The judge summed up the reason for the appeal being allowed in these words: 'We do not doubt the validity and value of DNA evidence in general. However... the effect of the evidence in the present case was to raise some arguable questions on whether the match probabilities put to the jury ... could properly be sustained...'

A search of the appeal reports for the 1990s brings up a number of similar issues. DNA was well understood; profiling from that knowledge was becoming an everyday matter in forensic laboratories. But as evidence in court, the recurrent problem of the material given by an expert witness was becoming apparent when DNA results were submitted. More recently, there have been similar theoretical problems with expert witnesses in such areas as paediatrics, psychiatry and even in sport science. But DNA is a different question: this is a precise art with astronomical figures relating to probability of guilt. But it has taken some time to resolve issues of how ideas of probability are presented in a criminal court.

The third case shows the confusions of the 1990s absolutely clearly, and again it concerned rape. In 1990, the appellant at the Appeal Court was convicted of rape and buggery and was given concurrent terms of eight years. The crime in question was horrendous: it was brutal, violent and merciless. The rapist had grabbed a widow who was about to go into her house, in November 1989, and he punched her, grabbed her by the throat and forced her inside. She was threatened with a knife, raped and robbed. The attack had been so vicious that a breast had been bitten and there was injury to the vagina and the anus. She never saw the face of her attacker, but the attacker left something – semen and pubic hair. The accused denied the offence and said he had been playing pool at the time and had then driven home. But his route home went past the location of the crime scene.

At appeal, the issue was entirely on the unsafe nature of the DNA evidence. This has been arguably the most complex case challenging DNA testing to date, certainly in cases of sexual assault. In the forensics lab, both single and multi locus profiling were used; it was explained to the court that the aim here was to produce the bands of the profile, multiply these and so work out the random occurrence ratio. That was the bone of contention. At first, the questioning of the main expert for the prosecution seemed conclusive:

Q What is the combination, taking the ratio into account?

A Taking them all into account, I calculate the chance of finding all of those bands and the conventional blood groups to be about 1 in 40 million.

Q The likelihood of it being anybody other than the accused?

A It is about 1 in 40 million.

Q You deal habitually with these things, the jury have to say, of course, on the evidence, whether they are satisfied beyond doubt that it is he. You have done the analysis, are you sure that it is he?

A Yes.

The law is rarely so simple and so straightforward, of course. As Benjamin Disraeli said, 'There are lies, damned lies, and statistics.' If a lawyer can create some doubt about statistics, then there is a hole in the solid foundation of the defence case. The issue here was whether the expert was right to multiply the findings of the results of the single locus test with the results of the multi locus tests. In simple terms, the experts disagreed. Research done at the time was brought in, conclusions regarding the dependability of the profile in a single locus probe. A statement by Dr Debenham from 1996 stated that

'Research studies have shown that some mini-satellites can be clustered together in close genetic proximity... The single locus probes, whilst separate with respect to each other may not be separate from the unknown mini-satellites detected by a multi locus probe.'

In other words, the profiles, expressed as the columns or bands with the distinctive pattern of the genetic material of the individual, may not be assumed to be the same all the way through the total material used to calculate the probability. It was a matter of maths.

Consequently, various experts debated the ratio of probability that the man in court was the rapist. Was the expert's action in multiplying the figures from the two tests 'legitimate' – the word used in the official court report. The experts working for the Crown conceded that they were not aware of any other usage of that testing; no proof existed of the reliability of the fact that the two testing methods produced independent results – and that there was a chance that the two testing approaches were dependent.

It was not a miscarriage of justice. The man making the appeal had served over half his sentence and was eligible for parole, and the judge ruled that a retrial would put the accused at a disadvantage if he tried to prove his alibi after such a passage of time. The appeal was allowed.

Long before these cases there had been a large body of literature addressing the issues related to expert witnesses in court. The first crime on record for which a witness gave expert scientific testimony was in Belgium in 1852 involving the chemist MJ Orfila and a man called Pare, a in murder case, that of, of Visart de Cocarme. The testimony was successful and was the determining element in the evidence. Lessons were gradually learned, and in 1981, before DNA began having a role in court, the American forensic scientist Joseph Bono summarised the established causes of controversy in this area as being the contrast been 'scientific truth' and 'legal truth' and the unavoidable conflicts between forensic scientists and lawyers. Bono foresaw the main problems as evident in the above cases, insisting that a well-prepared forensic scientist would be 'knowledgeable in his particular field as well as in the operation of the court'.

One thing that has happened more frequently since these 1990s cases with DNA is that there has been closer liasion between the lawyers and the experts.

Chapter 9

The Midlands Ripper
1993–2000

ince the Yorkshire Ripper years, there has been a link between serial killers and motor vehicles. Peter Sutcliffe was a lorry driver, and somehow, largely through the media frenzy around that case, the awareness of criminal opportunity for people working the major transport routes has been raised to the level of paranoia in the public and forensic expertise in the police laboratory. The reasons are not hard to find. Imagine the sense of freedom and opportunity of a criminal driving at night. Being in a car or lorry on one of our motorways creates a sense of invisibility. Moving in a pack, undetected within the flow of normality, suits the serial killer mentality perfectly.

Driving, particularly in the years before mobile phones were widely used, induces in the person in the car a sense of being beyond contact, outside the channels of communication; it also created instant mobility and the technology to change course, switch directions, take a chance for a killing, when the victim is in sight. If the driver is very familiar with the geography – the road routes from motorways to B roads – then that provides yet another predator scenario. With serial killers, we are dealing with predators of course; these people (mostly male) act like animal predators in a 'patch' – a territorial area in which they operate, developing a sixth sense for potential victims, a specific modus operandi and often a taste for a fetishistic sexual release.

Sutcliffe in West Yorkshire, masturbated over the corpses of victims; even before he killed he had a ritualistic set of murder apparatus and a method of attack that would maximise sexual satisfaction.

With the case that has become known as the Midlands Ripper we have all these elements. The victims were prostitutes, and eventually, even before the triumph of DNA in this case, the killings led to an intensification of the police initiatives in forming nationwide 'crime mapping'. After it was realised, mainly with the work of David Canter in mind, that the Yorkshire Ripper had operated within a circumscribed area with Bradford as the epicentre, it was noted that the location of victims furthest from his home address were more or less the same duration of a drive away.

Unfortunately, with the Midlands Ripper, now safely behind bars, this did not totally apply, though it was largely correct. The story begins in March 1993 when the naked body of Tracy Turner was found and a murder squad meeting was called to consider the offender profile, then written by Paul Britton, who wrote about the hunt for the Midland Ripper in his book, *Picking Up the Pieces*. Britton's profile described a man who knew the area very well; he was a manual worker who knew, as Britton put it, 'Not just the macro-geography, but the micro-geography. He knows it as a driver.' But this 'Ripper' was one who was most likely a loner with 'a poor record in heterosexual relationships'.

There had been another finding just before Tracy's death: it was Samo Paul. There was a pattern emerging, and the most remarkable feature of this was the location of the bodies. Samo's body was found long after her death, in a ditch by Stanford Road, Swinford. Both bodies had been found dumped on a roadside verge near agricultural land; both were left near gateways. But Paul Britton soon got to work on the 'macro-geography'. He saw that both locations were close to the M6, M1 and A5 trunk roads. One of the most unusual features of these murders was that there had been no arrangement of the corpses, no ritual vestigial remains; Britton was certain that the same man killed both women. Britton was sure that the killer had picked up the women in the West Midlands.

The profiler's memory then recalled other dead prostitutes and there was a feeling that there were potentially other victims of this killer. He recalled two other cases, one a prostitute taken from Bristol and another found at Dursely in Gloucestershire. Both bodies had been found near verges and hedges on rural roads. These cases had not been solved, and Britton remarked that it was worth checking for other cases with that profile between Sheffield and Bristol. In other words, today's M42 and A 38 would be the main links between the two 'killing fields' and Birmingham would be in the centre of it all. Britton wrote in his memoirs: 'The moment you have two or more prostitutes killed close together in time or in geographical space, the idea that there is another 'Ripper' out there takes on a very strong energy.'

Operation Enigma then began. This was one of the first steps taken towards what is now a database for violent crime analysis. The National Crime Faculty was founded just after these killings and the realisation that crime mapping was a significant weapon in the fight against serial killers. The aim was to create a fully integrated approach to investigation; underpinning this work is an ongoing research activity, gathering information and using the expertise of various specialists. The National Centre for Policing Excellence has an operations database, and this has variables covering the offence, victimology, verbal behaviour, forensic details and location patterns. Add to that the psychology of deviant behaviour and the tendency for there to be 'display' coding of materials at the murder scene, and there is a high level of sophistication involved.

But in 1993, with prostitute murders to solve, it was a tall order trying to find this very mobile and also extremely efficient killer. It did not take very long, however. Alun Kyte was a man with set nocturnal habits, and he liked driving as much as he enjoyed killing. His lifestyle as a serial killer involved staying at various guest houses around the Midlands, then after an hour of settling in, he would get in one of his many cars or vans and drive into the night, looking for victims. He knew the road network, as Britton had surmised, and he tended to travel around 80-100 miles from his hotel. That fits with the crime mapping profile very well, except that, unlike the Yorkshire Ripper, the base in this case was not a fixed, permanent home.

Police have since named twenty-one locations where Kyte spent some time and they know about at least seven of the cars he had used in his crimes; he existed by stealing goods from a DIY store and then taking them back for return sums, and he even used a store card to collect points – from goods he had stolen. But one of the strangest things, showing the general level of unawareness in the public, is that when he ran a mobile car-tuning service he would keep the cars for a few weeks before returning them to the owners, and of course he had been using them, so there would be a lot more miles on the clock: a fact unnoticed by the people when their vehicles were returned to them. As is usual with criminals after arrest and trial, a tracing of the life-pattern was put together, and it was also noted that he was an asthmatic and would have a considerable documentation on this at a number of hospitals. He had been a sickly youngster, doted on by his mother and sister. In truth, as the police said at the time of the trial, 'The file we have delivered on Kyte to all British police forces is already thick... such was his mobility that his name cannot be discounted from anything unless it can be shown he was in some other place at the time of the attack.'

In March 2000, Kyte, thirty-five, was jailed for life, convicted for the murders of Turner and Paul. But he had been noted before his actual arrest. He had been seen behaving suspiciously in the forecourt of a petrol station at Balsall Heath, near Birmingham. When approached and questioned, his explanation was facile in the extreme, as he claimed that he was a journalist working on a documentary on the red-light area of Birmingham.

He put on a performance on that occasion, even making a pretend phone call to an editor, and asking all kinds of questions about the murders in the area. He was then twenty-nine, a nomad; he existed by doing all kinds of work, from painting to car mechanics. He worked as a trucker after that, an occupation that suited his criminal activity admirably. But in 1997 he raped a woman in a flat in Bristol. The DNA sample from that scene linked him to the murder of Tracy Turner. It was a terrible attack, as he had sodomised a woman who then managed to run away and no doubt save her life.

Kyte was one of those killers who craved for attention; like others in prison he could not resist bragging about his exploits. It was while he was in jail for the Bristol rape that the DNA link to Turner was found. He had apparently talked about his killings while inside, saying that he had killed and dumped two prostitutes in Leicestershire. He had even said that Turner had laughed at him while they were having sex and that he had strangled her. He said to one fellow inmate that a man shouldn't pay for that kind of girl and that was why he had killed her. As one reporter noted in 2000, there was little in his life to suggest that Kyte would 'embark on such a grisly criminal career'. He was born in 1964 at Tittensor, Stoke-on-Trent, and he grew up in a normal suburban street in Rickerscote, Stafford. He left school with no career path in mind and did whatever work came his way. People who knew Kyte said that he was rarely seen with women, and that he would occasionally be seen just playing pool in a pub, not staying long.

The trial was held at Nottingham Crown Court, and not only was there DNA evidence, but there had also been a person who had seen a body in the back of a car very close to where Samo Paul's body was found. This was Betty Wilson, who drove past a Ford Sierra parked on a grass verge; she saw a man in the front trying to pull a hat over his face, and by his side was a woman 'sitting bolt upright... wearing a black dress'. Wilson said that the woman's eyes were open and that she had strange marks on her face.

The court was learning about a man with a profoundly unnatural and dangerous interest in prostitutes, and also a man whose arrogance and need for self-advertisement was obvious. He said that he could not even recall having sex with his victims, saying, 'According to the scientists the DNA is mine, which means I have had sex with her... You have casual sex. You meet people. You have one-night stands. You don't remember them. At the end of the day that doesn't make me a killer.' He could not explain the presence of his DNA in the cross-match, and said simply that he was not a forensic scientist and it was for the jury to decide.

Similarly, when shown a drawing of a man seen near to where Tracy Turner was found, all he could say was that he looked nothing like the drawing, commenting, 'The only possible similarity is my receding hairline.' Throughout the trial Kyte was emotionless and simply stared in front, while people in the public gallery reviled him. There was a unanimous verdict of guilty from the jury and Mr Justice Crane sentenced Kyte to life imprisonment, saying, 'You cruelly killed these two unfortunate women... you are plainly a very dangerous man.' The extent of this 'danger' may be seen in the statement by police regarding a reconstruction of the Turner killing by Central Television. Police now believe that the programme fed his need to kill and he did so just three hours after the film.

In fact, Kyte has boasted that he has killed twelve women, and in March 2000, DS Creedon of Leicestershire Police said that 'He craves notoriety. He wants to be elevated to Ripper status.' The fact is that there are three known attacks and then a gap of recorded offences until 1997 when he was caught for the rapes in Bristol. There are some years unaccounted for and police are looking at that gap.

We know much about how he worked: in 2000 an anonymous street-worker told the *Observer* about a meeting with the man. She had lived to tell the tale. The woman in question was working the Balsall Heath area, alone, one night, when Kyte came to her and offered £40 for sex. She said he drove her in a Maestro to the dark car park of Moseley Hall Hospital. She said that his voice was soft and 'reassuring'. But then he went to the back of the car and put an arm around her neck, pressing a Stanley knife against her. Although he told her to undress and to give him her money, she said she was pregnant and that seemed to change him. He told her to get out of the car and go. She went straight to the police and told her story.

Mistakes had been made in the investigations regarding the two women, and this was admitted by the police. It was mainly because the buccal swabs could have been taken from Kyte at an earlier date; but as one spokesman explained, 'Different systems were in place at the time.' Whatever the reasons, the man was a multiple killer and so mobile and elusive that he had plenty of time to scour the Midlands for victims, and he may even have gone further afield. It is hard to resist the feeling that even behind bars, he is today cultivating his image as a 'Ripper' – a paradoxically resonant and suggestive noun, somehow elevating a killer to the premier league of brutal and heartless murder.

It has to be said, with recent developments in mind with regard to the Tobin case (Chapter 16) that the work of Paul Britton is to be acknowledged, and surely that achievement (and others) has to go some way to exonerate him from the criticisms he sustained for the Rachel Nickell case in which there were mistakes. The point is surely that profiling is such a demanding and uncertain science that it will always come second best to the statistics and probabilities of such forensic tools as DNA. But in the case of Alun Kyte, Britton's work was absolutely right in the profile and report.

Today, crime mapping is well established. At the Jill Dando Institute of Crime Science, for instance, the study of crime mapping looks at most of the features that were so important in the Kyte case, including 'priority neighbourhoods' and 'prediction patterns of criminal activity': these were not entrenched in criminology at the time Britton worked, and that has to be recalled. Today we identify crime hot spots and produce pattern analysis. In 1993 the help offered by a profile had much more impact and indeed produced results. The Midlands Ripper pattern of locations and itineraries makes total sense now, with hindsight, as profiling, crime mapping and of course DNA matches, all come together to illustrate what the future of crime detection will be.

Chapter 10

By the Old Canal
Ian Lowther, 1977–2000

A great philosopher once said that 'most men live lives of quiet desperation'. This was a comment on the baffling nature of the inner life, and how this may relate to our actions. When it comes to criminal actions – even to the extent of murder – that desperation appears to find expression in anyone at any time and for any reason, such is the lack of logic involved in trying to understand some varieties of homicide. A Yorkshire murder recently solved by science illustrates this perfectly.

In August 1977, Mary Gregson had a cleaning job at Salt's Mill, Bradford. She had only to walk 600 yards to get to work, but on the day of her violent death, she was attacked on the towpath of the Leeds-Liverpool Canal, strangled with a ligature and her body thrown into the water. She had had some tea with her son and then waved goodbye, and just a short time after that she was dead. Strangely, a woman passing by had seen the killer standing over the body and she offered to help, thinking Mary had had a fall, but the killer said matters were in hand. Then he dragged Mary down the bank to the canal.

It had been a violent attack: Mary had been punched and sexually assaulted; she had put up a fight, and her dying had been most brutal, as there was evidence that her head had thumped the ground several times.

This was strange in many ways. After all, this is tourist country in parts; it is close to the village of Saltaire at one side, and not far from Kirkstall Abbey on the other. Of course, there are extensive dwellings close by as well; this is an industrial area, highly populated. The trawl for suspects at the time extended to over 8,500 interviews, and all police really had to go on was the one sighting of the killer, said to have 'a gormless air about him'. At the time, there was no DNA is use in forensics, so the main approach was to take blood samples. Blood grouping tests were done on stains by Mary's clothing. There was a major construction project going on close to Salt's Mill as a new base for the Inland Revenue was being built, and one of the men tested in 1977 was Ian Lowther, who was working as a labourer there. He was also a van driver, but he had been working at that site at the time; he had an alibi, and no previous convictions, so he was passed over. But in 2000, at Sheffield Crown Court, Lowther pleaded guilty to the murder of Mary Gregson. What had happened was that DNA techniques had advanced so far that a match was made from semen stains on the victim's body after a cold case review in late 1997. In 1985 a single locus profile had been unsuccessful as there was no material of sufficient quality to make that test possible; then in 1995 a more sensitive test was done, but still with no result. The reason for the triumph here was Low Copy Number (LCN) testing, as discussed in Chapter 5. But a recap is needed here.

LCN testing has allowed work to be done on materials with very low DNA profiles. There has been debate, as in the discussion of the World's End killings and the Manchester rape cases in Chapters 5 and 8, but in the Mary Gregson case, the evidence was incontrovertible. LCN has been in use since 1999 and has been refined. A speculative slide was made from two items of Mary Gregson's underwear which had been looked at before for blood grouping. On this slide, some sperm heads were found and so the knickers were sent for LCN testing.

Research had previously shown that a substance called cyanoacrylate could enhance marks and stains without affecting

DNA traces; if DNA material is shed on a touched surface (in this case the underwear) then enhancement methods have become possible. At first, it was found that on clothing, after a simulated assault, more of the attacker's DNA was found in specific areas of the clothing than that of the wearer. In the instance of an attack such as this by Lowther, as the body was placed in water, there were also deterioration factors. But what is known as 'secondary transfer' was notably subject to analysis: in plain terms, the hands of the attacker on the victim's underwear and the residual semen. The match was made between the profile found by LCN and the blood test taken earlier. This meant that the police were soon knocking on Lowther's door. He was still living in the same area, well liked by neighbours and apparently a likeable character.

The arrest was made in April 2000 when Bradford detectives arrived at his house in Baildon. Over thirty-two years had passed but a cold case had been resolved; plenty of the previous suspects had moved away, but the killer was just a few hundred yards away from the location of the killing. Reports at the time noted that he showed no emotion, and even put his slippers behind the door, ready for when he was to go home – but he never did return.

The story of the day of the murder began to emerge. He had been drinking heavily after finishing his shift at work - downing seven pints of beer. The case has been investigated by Yorkshire crime writer Andy Owens, and he has told the story of that fateful day. Lowther was living with his wife and daughter; he was just twenty-four, and under interrogation he revealed that the drinking had been done when he should have been at work. The reason for his walk along the canal was to try to walk off the effects of the beer, because he had to collect his little daughter from his mother-in-law's home. What happened then was defined by DCS Taylor, speaking to Andy Owens, who said it was 'a moment of madness'. It terms of motive, it was indeed a mystery.

All we know is that, in spite of Lowther's hazy memory of the attack, he had made advances to Mary and been refused. If it was a moment of madness, then it was something utterly in the category of the 'Mr Hyde' to his everyday 'Dr Jekyll'. If we add to that the fact that in the twenty years between the offence and his arrest, he had been living in close proximity to where he did the deed, and had also been totally 'clean' in terms of any criminality. In fact, he was divorced in 1999 and then lived alone in Baildon, where neighbours told Owens that 'There's nothing bad to say about him, other than he's a lovely man.'

We have the problem of accounting for this paradox: here was a man who would baby-sit for neighbours and live quietly, liking his own company, either reading or walking in the Dales; he was working as a driver when arrested and appears to have been a model employee. The situation we appear to have is one in which a man has done the most horrendous murder while being in possession of 'the demon drink'. Owens notes that he was thought of as a moderate drinker and that seven pints was well in excess of his usual tipple. But drink alone cannot answer the questions. Lots of quite normal, inoffensive people occasionally overindulge down the pub but do not tend to commit rape and murder on the way home.

In 1977, the lines of thought followed in the investigation make complete sense now, with hindsight. First, the nature of this murder has the hallmark of being by a serial killer or at least by an opportunist killer with a record of violent crime. Naturally, bearing in mind the developments in that area just after this murder with regard to the Yorkshire Ripper, it could have been one of his many other murders yet unknown. The other possibility was that the prime suspects would have been family members – simply because the murder statistics always lead the police to take that into consideration. The vast majority of killings are done by people who know their victims. Both theories came to nothing in 1977 and in the subsequent years. This is why a criminal profiler would find the case to be extremely hard to crack. In fact, police did employ a profiler when the case was re-opened. There was nothing in Lowther to fit any established profile.

What we do know about the man is that he was born in Harrogate on 29 October 1952, the younger of two sons born to a middle-class family; his father was a chauffeur and his mother was a housewife. When Lowther left school, at sixteen, he had no qualifications and so went to Harrogate Technical College, from where he was put on day release to Shipley College. He was married in May 1973 and the couple lived at Denby Drive, Baildon, later moving to a house in Central Avenue after the birth of their daughter. That is not, one might argue, a biography with any hint of a psychopathic personality. But then, much the same could be said of many serial killers.

Where this leads is to a consideration related more to abnormal psychology and the functions of the brain than to any serial killer trajectory found in his life. This was a one-off opportunist killing, and that phrase is used glibly, with the explanation of 'I could, so I did' being the logic of the motive. If we accept that the alcohol caused chemical changes in the brain and so the normal control of 'civilised behaviour' was temporarily switched off when he saw Mary walking on the canal, then we open up one of the oldest issues on legal defences. Well before the modern period and the more sophisticated definitions of personality disorder, murders done particularly by husbands on wives while in drink were never any kinds of events leading to a courtroom defence of insanity or diminished responsibility. Briefly, this means that the likelihood that here we have an opportunist murder done when restraint mechanisms were switched off. The killer's ordinary, equable and respectable life after the event provide evidence for this theory.

Lowther's later life supports the line of thought that sees him as a victim of circumstances rather than a person who wilfully makes things happen in the course of his professional life: he changed careers, becoming employed at British Mohair

Spinners in Baildon, and then, after redundancy, he worked for a print shop in Bradford, as a delivery driver. But just after his marriage and shortly before the murder, he was labouring. This all makes for a personality adrift in a world of circumstance: feckless and weak, with no imperative drive to create a social personality. Such a person lives a life of service and often subservience rather than a course of experience that is shaped to a desired aim. Of course, Lowther lived all those years close to the murder scene, and his interior life was a dark chamber, perhaps constantly awash with the images of remorse and self-effacement.

PC Eddy Gorney told Andy Owens that when he was a young policeman '... we'd never heard of DNA – the only testing was blood groups. It never occurred to me that you would be able to identify a person from their saliva.' But along came the most sensitive DNA testing technique to date, and a few old cells from degraded samples in this case led to the arrest. After an intelligence screening of all the men involved in the first investigation, the match was found.

In court, the prosecution barrister stated that Lowther had been the 532nd man seen that year by detectives. His buccal swab, taken in February 2000, meant that the chance of him not being the killer was one in a billion. Now, unlike the Manchester cases described in Chapter 8, the process of DNA evidence and statements of recurrence ration are more smoothly and unequivocally dealt with. The counsel for the defence could only explain the killing as 'ten minutes of total brutal madness' and pointed out that Lowther was a shy, quiet man.

Good, persistent police work and scientific expertise explain this late but impressive conviction: police in 1998 took 3,000 buccal swabs and they had their man in that trawl. For these reasons, the Lowther case will always be quoted as a notable success for the use of DNA profiling, but the mystery of the motivation, other than the obvious one of opportunistic mindless assault, may never be fully understood.

Chapter 11

'A Thirty-six Million to One Chance' Edward Hopkins 1995–1997

In September 1995, fifteen-year-old Naomi Smith left her home to post a letter. It was late at night, and she intended to return home immediately, but instead she walked down an alley, known as a jetty in the area of Ansley Common, Warwickshire, and stepped into a recreation area where she was to die.

She died violently and was raped in a most vicious way; we have a particularly detailed account of the investigation, and also of the scene of crime, because Paul Britton has written in detail about his involvement with the hunt for the killer. She was found with her throat slashed, her knees raised and legs apart, a savage bite-mark to one breast, and most horrendous of all was the immediate signs of a brutal assault with an object into her vagina. One of the most disturbing aspects of the case was that her body was found in this state by her friend and her father, who had gone looking for her. Her father described what happened: 'Outside the air was very dark and damp. Emma walked along the driveway situated some twenty yards to the left of our house which leads to the Rec and a small play area which had some swings and slides…As I got to the top Emma was running back to me, screaming and shouting. She was shouting my name and telling me to come quick...'

Imagining that scene is evocative of one of the very worst experiences a relative of a victim would dread: her father drove towards the 'Rec' as it was known, late at night, after his daughter had not returned from posting the letter, shone his headlights towards a play area and saw a white shape by the slide. It was the body of Naomi, and to cover her, to maintain some dignity, he covered her nakedness and turned her to one side – clearly not the best thing to do from the point of view of a scene of crime officer, but totally understandable. The wounds on her body were awful, but from the standpoint of the investigation, they were markedly seen as sources of good forensic evidence.

When the death was first reported, there was naturally panic and fear in the neighbourhood; Naomi had been stabbed as well as sexually assaulted, and people expected further attacks. It was the type of crime associated with a serial killer or at least, with some kind of maniac. The headmaster at Hartshill told the press, 'Naomi and her friend were always together at school. They did the same things and were inseparable. I would describe them as the closest of best friends almost to the exclusion of everyone else.' That friendship was to help Paul Britton assemble his profile of the killer, and everything he wrote for the police was to prove accurate when he was found.

Naomi's close friend, Emma, was interviewed by Britton and that meeting brought out what is now seen as a paradoxical aspect of the events at the time: the fact that Naomi was reported as being quiet and something of a loner, but then also other witnesses spoke of her being out late at night and in the early hours of the morning, wearing a short skirt and talking to passing drivers. In fact, what came out of Britton's interview was the kind of character profile all parents of teenagers would be familiar with – the kind of mix we find of what the child wants the parents to see and know and the other, hidden life. None of this helped in the trail leading to the killer, apart from the contribution made to Naomi's patterns of life and adoption of the community values around her, with her peers in particular.

In plain English, the community Naomi adhered to was exactly what could be found in any small town in England: teenagers gather anywhere where they can be together, talk and 'hang out'. Sometimes that involves subterfuge when it comes to keeping parents informed; less commonly it might involve alcohol, sex or drugs. Naomi was no different in that respect to thousands of other normal teenagers. But her lifestyle helped Britton to build the profile that really mattered – that of her killer. By asking questions about her and Emma's habits and little secrets, matters of sexuality were opened up, material that would fit well with a profile of a violent offender. Britton wrote: 'His track record is one of lack of awareness and unsophisticated relationships with girls. Although he has high sex needs, he lacks the refinement and wherewithal to find partners... Local venues will also feature in his masturbatory fantasies and he may have followed local girls ...' This is in line with thinking about the incipient stages of psychopathy and criminal behaviour. It was exactly right, as things turned out.

The investigation focused on sightings of Naomi in her last few hours of life. She was seen looking up the road, as if expecting someone and then turned into the alley towards the Rec. It was ascertained that she had been asked to check if her friend's car was parked outside her house, as it was planned that she could stay the night there. But various sightings were noted and one in particular was clearly, as we know with hindsight, a meeting with the killer. A boy described a tall young man who matched the description given by Edwin Hopkins when he phoned Bedworth police station after his mother had suggested that he call them. He said, 'I was in the area of Ansley Common that night. I am six foot tall with mousy blond spiky hair. I had a pushbike with me that night.' On the night of the murder a cyclist reported having to swerve to avoid hitting someone running from the Rec across the main road, saying, 'He was a white male between twenty and twenty-five, six foot tall with an athletic build and short blond hair that looked bleached…'

The young man who phoned the police was Naomi's killer. The net was closing in on him, and the success of this hunt was a triumph for three of the tools in crime detection: odontology, psychological profiling and DNA fingerprinting. The teethmarks left in the victim's breast proved to be a 'fingerprint' that individualised the killer as much as any fingerprint per se. Dr Andrew Walker, a forensic odontologist, said when giving evidence: 'I found that one of his [Hopkins'] front teeth was missing. The arrangement was unusual. As a result of the tooth loss the other teeth had moved into the space and closed the gap so that the upper jaw was lopsided. All the irregularities fitted the bite marks perfectly. It was a very good match.'

The psychological and police detective work had been accurate and logically correct, assuming that the killer was local. To make the testing easier, the DNA work had brought a positive profile to the armoury of detection, and a mass screening of buccal swabs was the next move. A particularly fascinating aspect of this investigation is the way that logic and statistics had to be used in order to make the screening work out in terms of the costing. Each buccal swab cost at that time £40. The budget for DS Bayliss was £40,000. If the profiler and detectives, along with some basic rationale of which men to choose could sort out a group to test, then the budget would be adequate. The target group in total was around 5,000 potential suspects – men between fourteen and forty living within half a mile of the crime location.

Computers came to the rescue. The HOLMES database was linked to a newly-created function called, logically, 'Watson' and this provided a methodology for reducing the population of potential suspects down to the most likely individuals based on a list of profile details. The first reduction took the figure down to 850. That meant that there was finance to back the operation. On 24 September, two weeks after the crime, the work began;

when news broke in the press about the DNA profile of the killer, and the so-called 'dragnet' of the screening was in the headlines, the detectives were full of confidence that they would get their man.

Backtracking on statements made to police in the course of the inquiry, there is a sequence of events from the night of the killing that may be put together. A woman stated that Hopkins called at her home and asked for some aftershave and shampoo, as he wanted a shower, and that was at around half past ten. Another person said that Hopkins had asked for shampoo and had also said, very late that night, that 'something had happened' down at the Rec at the Bretts Hall estate. Hopkins himself, when talking to the police, had made no secret of the fact that he knew Naomi and that he also spent time around the area of the Rec. He said, 'I used to play football and meet with all my mates... It's considered a general meeting place. I've not visited the Rec for at least the last six months...'

Hopkins lived with his parents, and he was working as a paint-sprayer. His alibi when first questioned was that he had been at his sister's house and that he had borrowed a bike to go to buy things from a local shop at nine-thirty. He said he had bought eight cans of lager and fourteen bags of crisps and returned to his sister's house by ten. Later, his sister admitted that he had been away for forty-five minutes and that when he had come back, he had been wearing different clothes. His excuse for his lateness was that he had been stopped for having no lights on the bike.

But the DNA evidence was incontestable; as well as the DNA there was the evidence from the teeth marks. What then came out was his past history. Hopkins indeed fitted the Britton profile: in March 1993 he had indecently assaulted a girl near the Rec. The story was that he had followed her, tripped her up, and then sat on top of her, after taking down her knickers, but then he had run away. This is perfectly in line with the trajectory of sexual predator psychopaths – the early phase of voyeurism, then touching and molesting, not being able actually to rape; then in the next phase the attacks become more serious and daring. In this instance the girl had not pressed charges and Hopkins had been merely cautioned.

Hopkins was one of the first few names to come from the computer when the swabs had been taken and matches searched for; when another test was done, this time on his blood, the DNA analysis again had a match to Naomi's body, linking with saliva. Despite the fact that the police had charged him and referred to the DNA evidence, Hopkins still argued that it could not have been him. He made no plea when he stood in the Magistrates' Court at Nuneaton, and then at Birmingham Crown Court on 22 January 1997 when he pleaded not guilty. But the apparently ordinary-looking youth living with mum and dad had another side to him, something in him that loved blades and repulsive weapons. He had machetes and knives hanging on the walls of his bedroom. The basic facts of what he had done came out lucidly in court, from his attempts to strangle her, through to the unspeakably brutal attack on her body, culminating in the instrument forced strongly into her vagina. Naomi's mother stated that she considered him 'evil' and added that, 'We do not call this justice. We are advocates of capital punishment.'

Hopkins was twenty years old when sentenced to life imprisonment. Mr Justice Tucker said, in sentencing, 'It was a savage murder and it had sadistic features. You are, in my opinion, a very dangerous young man... I sentence you to custody for life.' There is no denying that savagery: forensic reports stated that the force of the vaginal assault would probably have been enough to cause death. The barrister for the prosecution, Colman Treacy, said that the DNA found in the saliva on Naomi's body matched Hopkins' and that there was a 36 million to one chance of a match.

There is a sad irony in the comment made by one neighbour: 'Naomi was very popular in the area and would speak to anyone... she was very confident and very inquisitive. She would always be the first to go and have a look if anything was happening.' Beneath all the hype and media overstatements, there is a tale of a young girl who, in spite of her moderate school achievements and other minor problems such as a dead nerve on her face (which must have affected her self-image) was actually bright, curious, and wanted to experience life, wanted to socialise and communicate with people. That always involves trust, and she was desperately unfortunate in that a young man she trusted was a murderous psychopath with serious personality defects. Her friend Emma, who perhaps knew her better than anyone, has had to live with the trauma of that night. She said, in 1997, 'I saw what that evil person did to her. I don't think I will ever forget when I went to the Rec.'

Shortly after the trial, in the House of Lords, the Criminal Evidence (Amendment) Bill had its second reading and was soon to become law. Lord Taylor of Warwick explained the reason for the bill with reference to this case, 'Noble Lords will be aware of the horrific rape and murder of fifteen-year-old Naomi Smith and the part that DNA played in securing the recent conviction of her killer... This Bill has the potential to make a significant impact on the fight against crime. Its central purpose is to add the DNA profiles of some 7,750 serious violent sex offenders and burglary offenders who are currently serving prison sentences or are detained under the Mental Health Act to the national DNA database.'

It was noted at that discussion that 3,300 matches had been achieved through DNA profiles; the act even extended the power to take samples to 'certain other detained mentally ill offenders'. In other words, it was becoming acknowledged that the efficacy of DNA sampling could extend into the realms of preventive crime as well as in investigation and punishment. It was that bill which allowed for the taking of samples from people charged with offences, generally. In effect, DNA samples were equated with the routine taking of fingerprints.

A final reflection on the Bretts Hall case is that the area was the setting for George Eliot's 'novel of provincial life', *Middlemarch*, published in 1871-2. Eliot, real name Marian Evans, wrote the book to help readers understand the social upheavals at a time when radicals campaigned for political and social reform. In that novel people fall in love, fail in relationships, learn to change their lives. Parents worry constantly about their children and about their finances. Essentially, little has changed in that context, but we live in a world in which young people cannot walk out with safety in the late evening, and no parent can be so vigilant that they are oppressive and cramp their children's lives by constant vigilance. Eliot would not have understood that change, though there was plenty of violent crime in rural England in 1870, and people like Hopkins would have walked out onto a scaffold. If we try to write a similar 'study of provincial life' today then the restlessness and freedoms of young people figure in terms we cannot explain by traditional morality.

As with so many crime cases in which both the victim and the aggressor are young people, the depressing fact is that the psychological profiles involved often lead the public to see that the boundaries between 'violent crime' and 'mental sickness' are often blurred. We no longer have the concept of the 'criminally insane' and we have to accept that people such as Hopkins cannot function within the norms of everyday morality and civilised behaviour. What police work is now getting right is the formation of communication systems that will provide the back-up for such forensic work as DNA sampling. For instance, when DS Bayliss began his investigation, he used the National Computer Database known as CATCHEM, something started in Derbyshire by DCS Duncan Bailey. This played a prominent part in the arrest of Robert Black, another serial killer who specialised in the murder of young girls.

Chapter 12

The Lesley Molseed Case
1975–2007

There are some crime stories that should never be labelled as 'true crime' because that genre conveys the notion of a 'red and black' – a paperback about gangland or serial killers. There are some crime stories for which even the term 'crime' seems somehow inadequate. There are even stories which reach out beyond anything a plain documentary can achieve: they reach into the darkest recesses of the human soul and they raise questions about the fundamental nature of mankind. They remind us all that we are riddled with weaknesses, errors, ineptitude, malevolence and spite. These stories give a dark warning to anyone who thinks that a criminal justice system is always perfect and infallible.

This is the story of a man who was wronged in the extreme: a man who died aged forty-two in 1992, after going through hell on earth; it is also a story of a loving family whose pain can never go away; it has already cost one of them his life. It is also a story of how science can relocate a moral balance and a sense of justice, in a case that now has a closure. But the word 'closure' is the most powerfully ironic word in a story brimming over with cruel ironies.

In February 1975, Mr David Waddington QC and Member of Parliament, was awarded £40 a day in payment for his recordership. This meant that he could act as a part-time judge in a crown court. That payment was not conditional on 'the foregoing of any part of parliamentary remuneration'. Mr Waddington was to become Home Secretary later in his career. He was rich, part of a respected elite. He would have enjoyed sitting down to dinner that night, hearing about his additional wealth. As he went home to his very large home, study and welcoming domesticity, a tax clerk from Rochdale was entering Armley Jail. He was to be called 'Oliver Laurel' because he was as large as Oliver Hardy and as gauche and infantile as Stan Laurel. He was to be attacked and severely beaten, because the prison inmates thought him to be a murderous paedophile.

Mr Waddington was to defend the man after his remand period, at his trial on 7 July 1976. The alleged child-killer was Stefan Kiszco. This man was to be released in 1992, after serving sixteen years in prison for a crime he had not committed. The prosecution lawyer at the trial, Peter Taylor, became Lord Chief Justice the day after Kiszco was cleared at the Court of Appeal. Such are some of the principal ironies in a case that was eventually solved by DNA, with the real killer of the little girl put safely behind bars, for life.

The story began on 5 October in Rochdale, when Mrs Molseed asked her eleven-year-old daughter to go to the shop for a loaf of bread and an air freshener. Lesley was a sick child, very much underweight; she weighed only three stones, was small and had some learning difficulties. But little Lesley was a lovable child, clearly a daughter who was treasured by her family; her mother spoke of the girl as 'Very dainty... she had absolutely loads of friends. She was bubbly, full of life, full of the joys of living.' Lesley was 'a little imp' who loved her family life, and used to do housework to earn her pocket money. Before going out to the shops that night, she had joked that it should have been her brother, Freddy's job, so she could claim his money.

Lesley never came home. Mrs Molseed was making the Sunday dinner and everything seemed normal. Everything should have been like every other weekend: contented, routine, a happy family time and place. But roving the streets was a sadistic and twisted killer, and he saw Lesley, ideal prey for his deviant desires. A search for Lesley began and her body was not found until three days later, on the moors not far from home. She had been stabbed a dozen times, and although her clothes were still on her body, there were semen stains on her underwear.

What then happened was that some teenage girls reported a man who had allegedly exposed himself to them at around that time. One girl said that the man had been stalking her. The supposed flasher was Stefan Kiszco. He was certainly a young man with some eccentric personality traits, such as noting down car number plates of any vehicles he found irritating. Kiszco, who lived with his mother, was also ill, and his illness was something extremely relevant to this case. He had been having treatment for hypogonadism – a defect in the reproductive system that results in the testes not functioning, and not producing sperm. As the gonads produce sex hormones, a deficiency in that may have all kinds of side effects, including problems in using language, fatigue, atrophy of the muscles, poor sleep and a loss of bone mass. In other words not only was Stefan ill: he had symptoms which led to all kinds of related problems, including depression and poor communication. In short, in a community of 'normal' people there would be some who would ridicule him and use him as a target to ease their own insecurities. The three girls who accused him of 'flashing' and shadowing them were lying, as they later admitted.

To make things worse, it is now well documented that this man, easily frightened and bullied, made a 'confession' to police. When he explained why he confessed to this murder he said that although he had never even met the little girl, he was terrified, and he said that he, 'Started to tell these lies and it seemed to please them [the police] and the pressure was off as far as I was concerned … I thought that if I admitted what I did to the police they would check out what I said, find it untrue and let me go...'

Anyone familiar with the hit television cop drama, *Life on Mars* will be thinking that for Stefan, there were real-life equivalents of DCI Gene Hunt and his old-time investigation techniques, for which the word 'suspect' was invariably equivalent to 'culprit'. Crime historians may easily prove that in the 1970s there were severe problems in the prison service and in the police in terms of 'canteen culture'. It was a period in which the repression of crime and offenders was perceived largely as an unrelenting belief in the corrupt nature of Joe Public when drunk, politicised or radical. Penology was focused entirely on punishment and retribution rather than rehabilitation and treatment. A man like Stefan would be a figure who also fitted the prejudices about sexual deviance at the time.

For instance, in September 1976, a sex offender was jailed at Leeds Crown Court for four years, and was given treatment to suppress his sexual drive. A psychiatrist, Dr Hugo Milne, said that the drug cypro-sterone, which had been used only for the previous two years, worked by taking away all 'sexual drive'. This was a case in which a man had indecently assaulted a young girl, and the media time and space given to the use of the drug in such cases served to increase the public opinion that 'perverts' had to be drugged and shut away. Stefan was compared to that and classified accordingly; his treatment for the hypogonadism would have been seen by many as a freak of nature, relating him to the inevitable deviance for which he was cruelly tormented.

Stefan had been a patient at Birch Hill hospital not long before the Molseed murder; he was then transferred to Manchester and there the endocrinologists diagnosed the problem. He had an alibi as well, being with his mother, visiting his father's grave in Halifax at the time of the killing. But after the 'confession' things were made much worse in court by the fact that he claimed manslaughter. This approach of 'riding two horses' could only serve to move all ground of reasonable behaviour from under him in the eyes of the jury. First, he had confessed to the killing and second, in claiming manslaughter, the implication was then that the alibi had been a lie.

At Leeds Crown Court, after over five hours of discussion, the jury found Stefan guilty of murder by 10-2. He was given a life sentence and the ironies piled on again in the narrative of this arguably most celebrated miscarriage of justice: this is because the judge complimented not only the police for their good work, but also the girls who had claimed Stefan had exposed himself to them. The prosecution had put before the judge and jury a portrait of a man who could have been interpreted as a strange deviant who was capable of iniquity as well as eccentricity. After all, any matter of perceived deviance in conformist times can be seen as very close to being something else. In 1976, definitions of sexual behaviour, in spite of the moral liberation of the Swinging Sixties, were very much maintained with reference to a high level of general ignorance in matters of biology and indeed of the English language. In 2005, many years after this prejudice, during a moral panic based on a case of paedophilia, a paediatrician was victimised and attacked because the gang of neighbours in question confused the two words.

There are two remarkable features of this case which, looking back with full knowledge of the circumstances, were not prominent in the trial: first, that Stefan Kiszco's semen had no sperm, and second, that he had broken his ankle shortly before this murder, and the murder had taken place on high ground. The overweight and lame Kiszco could hardly have handled that. But it is outrageous to note that at the trial there was no mention of the broken ankle and nothing said about the effects of the hypogonadism. The judge said, 'Children are a lot safer now that this monster has been put away.'

At this time, there had been a high-profile media coverage of a scandal at HMP Wakefield concerning its control system. For two years previous to Stefan's arrival there in the summer of 1976, violent and political prisoners there had been subject to the effects of Rule 43 – isolation of prisoners for various reasons. The prison service, under the pressure of protests and expert opinion from psychologists on the effects of isolation in prison, had scrapped the control system just before Stefan arrived, but they still kept him under the Rule 43 provision. Stefan was viciously attacked by six prisoners in jail; they punched and kicked him and injured him so severely that he could not walk for several weeks. It is not too melodramatic to say that prison officers saved his life.

In prison culture, it is well documented (and I have known this from personal experience) that so-called 'nonces' – sex offenders – are hated and reviled by the everyday criminals who rob, assault, defraud or kill other citizens. The moral code of male prisoners, strongly reinforced in the gangland books and biographies of famous thugs, is one with strict negative ideologies, such as respecting women ('the weaker sex') and never transgressing lines of demarcation with regard to supposed traditional British family life values. In other words, sex offenders are legitimate prey. Observation of a line of 'nonces' walking from a wing to an exercise yard conveys the sense of concern for security and protection in the ranks of the officers – who do a very difficult job in this context. In 1976 this moral code was even stronger, when there were more 'business criminals' around the prison establishment. Stefan was attacked a second time, in May 1977, and he needed several stitches to a head wound he had sustained.

Clearly, as time passed there were moves made to launch an appeal. In 1978 an attempt was made but this was rejected and after that the Stefan Kiszco story takes a turn for the worse: he became schizophrenic and had delusions. It has been pointed out that some medical opinion at the time considered this to be an instance of a man having 'delusions' of innocence. In fact, the trajectory of Stefan's prison life follows a pattern still evident today. A person incarcerated for a sex offence is asked to attend a course of treatment, a Sex Offenders' Treatment Programme.

Agreeing to that means that the prisoner has implicitly stated that he is guilty of a sex crime. I have worked, in the capacity of a writer, with men convicted of sex offences, and today the same 'Catch 22' dilemma faces them as faced Stefan. A truly innocent person in jail who refuses this course of treatment will then be considered to be not only guilty, but without remorse, and so the cycle of negative definition goes on.

Stefan was shunted from prison to prison until with his mental health giving real cause for concern, he was taken to Ashworth Hospital, and it was not until 1984 that anything significant happened regarding his appeal. His mother contacted lawyer Campbell Malone, and he and Philip Clegg sent a petition to the Home Secretary – but here is another irony – the new person in that job was Mr Waddington. So there was a delay in the appeal procedure until he moved on and Kenneth Baker responded. At last the case went to the Court of Appeal in 1992. Then the point was made that Stefan Kiszco could not produce sperm, and that the sperm on Lesley's underwear could not have been from him. He was cleared and almost immediately released. There were many people who needed to offer at the very least some kind of apology for previous statements and attitudes; some did and some did not.

In the Kiszco side of this tale, the end was that, only a few years after release, Stefan died, and his mother died shortly after that. They had been awarded £500,000 in compensation, but saw only a small first payment from that sum. Stefan, understandably, withdrew from the community and his health deteriorated further. The man who had been a powerless victim of a penal system as well as of extreme injustice, died of a heart attack just before Christmas 1993.

The coda to this part of the Lesley Molseed story is that the police were cleared of any wrongdoing in 1995; there had been ironies and odd circumstances in the Stefan Kiszco story from the beginning; even his murder trial was delayed in 1976 because prison officers had refused to take remand prisoners to court because of a dispute about overtime pay. This was a further cruel twist. If we examine some details of the first police investigations, it emerges that there were leads, and these were announced, but these fell away into nothing when Kiszco came along. For instance, in October 1975, detectives told the press that they were looking for a 'car like a patchwork quilt'. *The Times* reported that 'They emphasis that the car, which was seen at Denton, Manchester, when a girl aged six was assaulted on Tuesday, cannot be linked directly with Lesley Molseed's death.' They were trying, and the desperation at not having made any progress, was leading to the errors that tend to happen in frustration.

When the arrest was finally made, the press were keen to tell the public that Stefan used Lesley like 'a sex object' and then that he was 'having a sex hormone' given to him. The recipe for a 'monster' was there and of course influenced the men in the jails waiting for Stefan to arrive.

The Molseed story leads to a resolution; this is because DNA evidence was waiting for a man who kept a comic shop when finally arrested in 2007. Ronald Castree said that he had been expecting a visit from the police about Lesley 'for years'. He had been a taxi driver in the Rochdale area at the time of the murder; some months after killing Lesley he had abducted another young girl and taken her to a derelict house, but she had escaped. A picture then emerged of this man, a killer who had been 'underground' and beyond detection for decades but who now had been tracked down by DNA matching.

Castree had been arrested in 2005 and a buccal swab taken. Naturally, this was in the system and a match with the DNA in the semen on Lesley's knickers was found. Castree was on trial at Bradford Crown Court for the murder in October 2007, and Julian Goose for the prosecution pointed out that the DNA evidence made it a billion to one chance that Castree was not the killer. He was convicted for life. In court, it was said that Lesley had had a hole-in-the-heart operation and her weakness made the killing all the more heinous. Castree responded to the charge by saying, 'I had expected this years ago.' He denied the crime, and he spun a yard about being assaulted by police after a 1979 burglary, claiming that in revenge for him threatening to prosecute, he would be 'framed' for the Molseed murder. He also tried to claim an alibi, saying he was visiting his wife in hospital, but that was hopeless. The judge said that Castree should serve at least thirty years before being considered for parole; he is (in 2009) now fifty-six.

Of course, there was a defence, and this related to the DNA evidence. The claim was that the traces had been contaminated. Thirty-one years had passed, and so there could, it was suggested, have been 'cross-contamination' in the time of the storage of the DNA from Lesley's clothing. In 2007 Switalski's solicitors, acting for Castree, approached Forensic Access with regard to the possibility of DNA cross-contamination. Professionals from the Forensic Access team went with Castree's lawyers to the scene of the 1975 murder. The account of this, posted on the website of Forensic Access, also has an example of basic forensic scene of crime work that should have been done all those years ago:

> *The original allegations were that Stefan Kiszco had carried Lesley's body from the road, up a hill onto open moorland. When we visited the scene it was very evident that Mr Kiszco, who was not a fit man and had a broken ankle at the time, could never have carried the body of an eleven–year-old girl up to this hill –it took all of us a lot of energy to get up the hill, with nothing to carry... It is a tragedy that this scene was not examined in this way...*

Then, as to the DNA work, what happened was that the DNA evidence against Castree was from a 'tapelift' from Lesley's knickers. Because this item is simply a piece of sticky tape, the obvious fragility of that led the lawyers for Castree to ask about its reliability and how it could have been contaminated. Forensic scientist Roger Robson worked on the case.

It has to be recalled that in 1975, DNA played no part in forensic work for police investigation. But items of clothing were kept, and Robson, together with Clare Stangoe and Ted Kinner, knew how to work with the vestigial remains of the case records. A meeting was held with the lawyers and a strategy put together. In a newsletter called Benchmark, in 2008, the next step was described: 'Roger and Clare had to try to understand how Castree's DNA could have been transferred to a sticky strip that had DNA from the clothing (destroyed in the 1980s) – was this due to contact between Lesley and Castree, or to contamination in the forensic laboratory?' This might seem like splitting hairs in terms of the defence counsel for Castree – desperation in effect. But the fact is that in court, the slightest doubt about evidence can blow a case out like a house of cards coming down.

The scientists had to go to Wetherby, where the Forensic Science Service labs are, and look very closely at the location and the general procedures for materials and fabrics in cases like these. Their findings were vital to the success of the prosecution of Castree. First, they confirmed that just the one lab was used with the materials from the case; no precautions were taken to avoid DNA contamination (because DNA was not used!) and that the tapes had been opened and closed, and so could have been contaminated. As Castree had been busy attacking and having some kind of sexual contact with various females in the intervening years, the question arose: could his DNA from other procedures in the lab have contaminated the sticky strip from Lesley's clothing?

The report on this given to the court was obviously very important. Opinions had to be given, and in terms that the jury could comprehend. It was a procedure to admit that such contamination was theoretically possible, but the high improbability of such a thing has to be stated. In the end it was the recurrence ratio of a billion to one that led to the conviction.

It was a disturbing and emotional trial; the jury were given black and white photos of the murder scene, and also of the Turf Hill estate where both Lesley and Castree had lived in 1975. The revolting nature of the attack was described yet again, as if history had been re-enacted, even down to the details of the dozen stabbings on the girl's body and the note that the wounds were made with such force that, as Mr Goose for the prosecution said, 'The knife hilt or the killer's hand, had caused bruising.'

Of course, there is an entire and engrossing narrative attached to the case when we consider Stefan's family, and indeed Castree's too. In the early stages of the reporting on the case, 'medical experts' were called in to give their opinions, so that, for instance, one report in 1976 had the story that 'male sex hormone can induce exhibitionism'. In other words, the papers took what they thought the public wanted to hear about so-called 'perverts', stating, ' ... it is in such psychological abnormalities that injections of testosterone can induce sexually abnormal behaviour such as exhibitionism and sexual interest in young girls'. It is in reports such as this that we can just begin to see what pressures Mrs Kiszko was under at the time.

Even later, when the outrageous truths of the police investigation were revealed, there were still astounding reports, such as the news that the doctor who helped to free Stefan was sacked by the police; Dr Edward Tierney was no longer required. He had been a police surgeon for twenty-three years when he was told to go. He said that the police authority were not 'required to justify their actions to anyone'. Dr Tierney told reporters that he was 'merely thanked for the years of service' he had given. He was still 'mystified' in 1992 as to why samples he had taken from Stefan at the time were never presented as evidence. Tierney repeated the basic information that should have been decisive: 'The police knew that Stefan was infertile so he could not be the girl's killer.'

The detailed biography of Stefan given by Jonathan Rose in

1997 helps to explain some of the terrible prejudice surrounding
the man who came to be labelled a 'gentle giant'. Rose and
others wrote that Stefan, born in Rochdale, came from a family
who had fled Eastern Europe at the end of the Second World
War and come to Britain as refugees. Stefan's father, Ivan, died
in 1970, and Stefan was very profoundly affected by that,
becoming even closer to his mother, and being very dependent
on her. He managed to work at the tax office and his
eccentricities attracted attention, of course. Rose wrote: 'He had
a high-pitched voice and almost inevitably, did not have a
girlfriend. His teeth were brownish because of his near-
addiction to sweets, which he always carried in his baggy
trouser-pockets.' Rose tellingly wrote that 'local children always
found the meek Stefan, with his slightly popping eyes and
splayed feet, a figure of fun. He waddled down the street like a
bloated Charlie Chaplin. It was well-known that Stefan had
never harmed another living thing.'

Castree is in prison for life. The reason for that is that a piece
of forensic sticky tape had been kept in a laboratory for almost
thirty years. Since that momentous event, the analyses have
come forward on him, even in a television documentary shown
in 2008, in which it was said that he was 'weird in the bedroom
department' and that he wanted his lover to 'dress up in
schoolgirls' uniforms'. This man, who once ran Arcadia Comics
in Ashton-under-Lyme, was said to have been 'very jumpy
through the years' as he waited for what he sensed was the
inevitable visit from the police. Without the efficiency of the
forensic science lab and the energy and determination of
Campbell Malone and Philip Clegg, that knock on the door
from the killer's nemesis would never have come.

Chapter 13

Rachel Nickell and Robert Napper
1992–2008

On 18 December 2008, Robert Napper was sentenced to spend the rest of his life in Broadmoor Hospital for the murder of Rachel Nickell on 15 July 1992. That spare, factual sentence has brought to a closure a saga of profiling, investigation, miscarriage of justice and recriminations about policing perhaps unequalled in modern murder investigation. In the few days after the trial of Napper, the newspapers were packed with wise, reflective articles on the case and on the wider issues it opened up for discussion. At the heart of the trial was a profound criticism of offender profiling within murder investigations, and that has provided a spin-off story from the murder of Rachel that has in some ways provided as much intrigue and complexity.

Richard Edwards, in the *Daily Telegraph*, raised the question, 'Will we ever get inside the criminal mind?' His question made the assumption that there is a 'criminal mind' which may be defined, measured and handled as we might deal with a sack of flour. He even got his facts wrong when he wrote that profiling was still used in murder enquiries, but essentially he produced a critique of the subject which was long overdue. The media and the true crime press have raised offender profiling to a level of mystique that makes the so-called 'crackers' (after the television programme with Robbie Coltrane) seem like superhuman brains with the twisted empathic instincts of the killers they hunt.

David Canter, the man most associated with 'crime mapping' also responded to the Napper committal. His conclusions rightly pointed to the need for the police forces to get in step with the darker reaches of forensic science. In the armoury of the forensics lab, such exact sciences as fingerprinting, dating of bones, analysis of poisons and so on, can never be equated with the psychological knowledge employed by profilers. The latter is concerned with both human motivation and deviancy. It has to try to understand individuated fantasy as well as personality theory. David Canter wrote that, 'We still expect senior police officers to be generalists, turning their hand to crowd control one day and murder enquiries the next. Their expertise is seen as being police officers rather than in specialist knowledge of a particular field.'

The Napper conviction prompted these reflections because of the false imprisonment of Colin Stagg, and as we have detailed information about the 'honey trap' approach used to investigate him, from Paul Britton's book, *The Jigsaw Man*, most of the narrative of that miscarriage of justice are well known. But once again, the ultimate triumph, and the establishment of the truth of the matter was provided by DNA matching. In order to understand what happened that led to the trial and conviction of Robert Napper, we must go back to the basic facts of the case.

Rachel Nickell was a young mother and former part-time model; she was beautiful, lively and very happy in 1992 as she went for a walk on Wimbledon Common with her young son, Alex and their dog, Molly. She had lived a happy family life with her partner, Andre Hanscombe, and we know that she was very much fulfilled and enjoying life when the most horrendous attack on her happened. She was murdered, being stabbed forty-nine times, raped and was almost decapitated. Her little son was found clinging to her body, covered in her blood. The two detectives leading the hunt for the killer consulted Paul Britton, a profiler who had vast experience in clinical and deviant psychology, to help. The circumstances of the killing had a number of very rare aspects. The sheer extent of the mutilation and the savagery of the attack, including anal rape, seemed to indicate a deep mental sickness in the perpetrator. The police at the time were accustomed to dealing with the kinds of rapes and sexual assaults that happen opportunistically, but this had the hallmarks of something very different.

Britton has written about what happened next with sensitivity and caution. He was approached with the suggestion that, as there were suspicions about loner Colin Stagg who lived close to the Common and who had been around the scene at the time, it might be fruitful to use a 'honeytrap' method to bring out any culpability in him. This became known as Operation Exdell. Britton was aware from the start that such an approach might be illegal and that the resulting information about Stagg could be inadmissible in court. But he was assured that it was legal. The notion of a covert operation made Britton respond with some caveats about the probable outcomes as well, but he believed that the truth could be elicited by indirect means: 'As their mutual trust seemed to grow, the officer would gradually disclose more of his history which would include serious violent sexual crime. This would help to create an environment where the suspect could feel safe and even boastful in revealing his own background...'

But what was happening, though it was not seen at the time, was that Stagg, being a man who exemplified the kinds of sexual fantasist who has a streak of violence in the dream, was being interpreted as a psychopath. Britton was aware that there are male fantasies involving the domination and exploitation of women – as in the top-shelf magazines in newsagents – and he gave the opinion on several occasions that there was a massive difference between the inner fantasies of a shy loner who found relationships with women difficult, and a serial rapist who liked to slash victims in a frenzy. Reading Britton's account of the honeytrap ploy it is not difficult to see that he was flattered by the attention of the detectives and the experience of being valued in such a high-profile case. He wrote that the first two officers selected to take part in the trap, a man and a woman, were from the Yard's special unit, SO10, 'one of the most secretive units in law enforcement'.

But credit is due to Britton in that once the preparation for the trap was underway, he had the ability and the imagination to work with the female officer (known as 'Lizzie James' in *The Jigsaw Man*) to such an extent that we have the feeling that he was taking his own psychological theories in to the arena of applied criminology – not only theorising and offering a profile of a person, but building in behavioural features in a 'model' of investigation. In other words, he perhaps thought that the practical police work here had provided him with a way to test out the theory with interchanges and recordings of a real psychopath. This was all wrong-headed, but the appeal of that is totally understandable to anyone with a belief that their studies in criminal behaviour are for beneficial ends. After all, everyone involved in Operation Exdell thought that there was a high probability that Stagg was the killer of Rachell and they desperately wanted to 'get their man'.

Between Stagg and the officer posing as Lizzie there were letters and phone calls, and on several occasions Stagg stated that he had not killed Rachel despite his interest in, and knowledge of the case. But on one occasion he seemed to express knowledge about Rachel's body that only the killer would have known. It was clearly disturbing to the detectives at the time that their man had sexual fantasies about sex in open-air locations, but arguably the turning-point in this plan, which led to Stagg being charged was his knowledge of the crime scene. Britton wrote, after Stagg's account of Rachel's position after death, 'This description graphically and precisely matched the condition of Rachel's anus, yet from examination of the single photograph labelled KP27 [a photo shown to Stagg by police] Stagg couldn't have known such detail unless it was a guess.'

With hindsight and having had time to absorb the profile of

Stagg, it makes sense that he was the kind of fantasist who is always reserved, always withdraws into unreality and somehow freezes at the stage of voyeurism and a strangely offensive imaginative narrative of giving pain in sexual congress. He once said to 'Lizzie': 'I am not a murderer, as my belief is that all life from the smallest insect to plant, animal and man, is sacred and unique…' Yet this is the same man who claimed to have done a murder in Hampshire – something checked out by police and found to be nonsense. The string of details about Stagg and the Nickell murder include his incredibly close geographical knowledge of the Common, his supposed love of nude bathing and masturbation in public (not proven); his more than common interest in the murder, his odd beliefs and practices, and sightings of him by various witnesses in the area near the time of the murder, apparently behaving strangely. All this does not make a murderer. Britton also explained why he thought Stagg was the likely killer: 'This was such a rare kind of sexual deviance that the chances of two people sharing these characteristics and being in the same place at the same time, other than a special hospital or a prison, were extremely small. More importantly, his behaviour during the course of the covert operation had been exactly as predicted for this very unusual person.'

Unfortunately, as we now know, the real killer was a schizophrenic psychopath, and therefore is markedly different from a man who had extreme though not dangerous fantasies. This does expose the weaknesses of the art of profiling – perhaps an empathic art rather than a science?

Stagg was first the subject of a first hearing, then a trial for the murder after fourteen months on remand. At the Old Bailey trial he was acquitted and the covert operation was seen as exactly what some feared it would be – a failure. The results in all quarters were sadly very regrettable. 'Lizzie James' left the police and sued for damages; Stagg has received massive compensation; Britton's position is open to debate. Arguably, he did what he thought would be productive at the time. Rachel's partner has written on the case, and also Mr Justice Ognall, who dismissed the case, commented: 'I would be the first to acknowledge the pressures on police but I'm afraid this behaviour betrays not merely an excess of zeal but a blatant attempt to incriminate...'

Stagg's compensation was announced in January 2007, and by August 2008 it was announced that the amount had been stated by Lord Brennan – the figure being £706,000. Stagg has been keen to write his side of the tale, and has been involved in the production of two books which set out to explain what he has been through. The failure of the case against him was summed up by Harry Ognall in December 2008: 'There was no identification, no scientific evidence, no circumstantial evidence, and no subsequent incriminating behaviour. Neither was there DNA available to implicate or exonerate him...'

Then, in November 2004, Napper became the prime suspect for the murder. He had been already sent to Broadmoor for the killing of Samantha Bisset and her four-year-old daughter, being committed there in 1995. The Scotland Yard murder review group looked again at the case and the new DNA tests were applied (Low Copy Number). Work was begun on Rachel's clothing. Finally, in December 2008, after DNA testing by LGC Forensics, it was explained that the breakthrough linking Napper to Nickell was the match between a sticky tape from Rachel's son at the scene to paint flakings on Napper's tool box. There was also a footwear mark at the scene which matched Napper. At first, there was no DNA evident on the sampling, but a second attempt revealed both the DNA of an unknown male and the victim's. As Dr Angela Gallop has written on behalf of LGC:

'Further work on the unknown DNA established that the result was more than 1.4 million more likely if the DNA had come from Robert Napper then someone else unrelated to him. The DNA results, combined with the paint and footwear evidence provided compelling scientific evidence of Robert Napper's involvement with Rachel Nickell's killing.'

Working at the labs at Culham near Oxford, a team of more than twenty scientists under Roy Green took part in what has proved to be a momentous piece of forensic work. To back this up, markings on an A-Z map also relate to places of Napper's previous assaults. Hilary Bradfield, a reviewing lawyer working with the Crown Prosecution Service, has written that 'Robert Napper has at last accepted that he killed Rachel Nickell and the two psychiatric reports which were prepared for the prosecution and the defence are clear that he suffered from an abnormality of mind, which substantially impaired his responsibility at the time...'

Angela Gallop explained, talking on BBC radio, that they started the work on the cold case by studying the photographs showing the exact position in which Rachel's body had been found. Then a scientist was dressed in a similar way to the way in which Rachel was dressed; another scientist dressed similarly and inked his clothing, so that the exact parts of the clothing which should have had traces was located. A taping from that was re-analysed and this had Rachel's DNA and the DNA from 'an unknown male'. The scrap of paint was noticed later; the police were then asked to send all kinds of materials from Napper to the lab. That is where the tool box was studied. The paint fragments on that gave them the match. There was also a challenge involved in the footprint; at first it seemed too large to match Napper's but then, when a shoe of his size was placed in the same muddy ground, the suction of the pull out of the mud made the same distorted outline as the print at the crime scene.

The headline in *The Times* for 19 December 2008 read: 'Rachel Nickell's Killer is linked to 109 Sex Crimes'. There is now speculation that Napper has to be considered in relation to the deaths of Claire Tiltman, Penny Bell and Jean Bradley. There are notable similarities here; Jean Bradley died of more than thirty knife wounds, and Mrs Bell was killed shortly after that murder, being knifed fifty times while in her car. Between 1989 and 1992 Napper committed a series of rapes in south east London, usually with a knife, and it is now reckoned that over a hundred other similar attacks may be down to him. After questioning in 1992 regarding these rapes, he gave a blood sample but went into hiding after that. Just a month after that, Stagg was arrested. In May 1994, Napper was arrested and charged with the murder of Samantha Bisset and her daughter. Samantha had been stabbed and mutilated; she was killed near the front door and dragged into her lounge. Her daughter had been stripped, sexually assaulted, then put back to bed, before being smothered with a pillow. Napper certainly has a fixation with young mothers and their children; he rented a room on Plumstead High Street and from there he stalked, raped and killed.

Napper was a paranoid schizophrenic; in his childhood he had extra help for coping with Asperger's Syndrome. He was the eldest of four children, and his father told journalists that all four children in the family were taken for help and advice to a psychiatrist. Robert bullied his own family, even shooting a brother in the face with an air pistol. A fellow pupil is on record as saying that no one wanted to sit next to Napper in class: 'He was teased a lot about his spots… In a game of football once when he headed the ball, the game stopped because no other boy would go near the ball after it had touched his forehead. He left school at sixteen, with good academic qualifications, but did several jobs, basically drifting. At nineteen, he was in trouble with the law after being caught carrying a loaded gun. He also confessed to his mother that he had raped a woman at Plumstead, when he was twenty. She called the police about it, but they found nothing related to the confession, but apparently, according to a report in the *Guardian*, a woman had indeed been raped, in her own home, and in front of her children. He had gone into her house carrying a Stanley knife and wearing a mask.

The familiar question about such serial killers was asked in all kinds of places – how did he slip through the net of the law so many times? One answer is that there were other suspects for the crimes he had committed. Another might be that there was a very elaborate and internalised plan of campaign in his twisted mind and that meant that although he took some risks, he was also furtive, quick to slide into the night, and hide himself in apparent normality. When eventually his belongings were found and studied, it was observed that his A-Z from which he logged the attacks, had notes, such as 'sodden filthy bitch' and 'cling film on the legs'. In a dictionary in his possession, some key words from his sick mental landscape were marked – words such as 'necropolis' and 'carcass'. One note was perhaps the most chilling, referring to the Nazi doctor, Mengeles, who was involved in the cruel experiments in genetics and surgery during the Holocaust years. Napper has been disowned by his mother: she has burnt all photographs of him. His name will now be a regular in books and articles on 'sexual serial killers'. He had conducted a reign of terror across a broad sweep of London, a man with a knife in the dark, always hunting, watching, pouncing on the chosen victims.

Perhaps the comment that most sums up the reason for the length of Napper's reign of terror is from Professor Laurence Allison of Liverpool University, and his remark carries a profound irony with regard to the operations of profiling at the time of Rachel Nickell's murder: 'Frenzied, random, motiveless knife attacks on women are rare. Even more unusual are frenzied, random knife attacks on women with their young children present. Here was Britton with two of them under his nose and no one noticed.' It is too harsh a criticism of Paul Britton, and I feel that we could substitute 'the detection team' for the profiler. His attempts to help were clearly considered at the time. It was arguably that such a rare occurrence was there, but both were apparently localised. There was no lateral thinking which related the rapes around Napper's patch to Wimbledon Common at the time – and after all, there was a main suspect, and reasoning was focused on him, to the exclusion of others. That seems, with the wisdom of time passed and lessons learned, to have been a huge mistake, but we could say, *autre temps, autres moeurs*, or as LP Hartley famously said, 'The past is another country. They do things differently there.'

The killer of Rachel Nickell and many other victims as yet unknown can now safely turn his deathly fantasies on his own dark imagination, where his metaphorical knife can only harm that fragile inner space of sickness within him. The lives he has ruined are to him 'unreal' – merely fleeting images that broke in on his sick world. Recriminations and blame serve little purpose now, and it has to be hoped that lessons have been learned. With the increasing sophistication of DNA testing it is to be hoped that the war against the killers in the shadows will turn in favour of the forces of law.

Chapter 14

An Axe Through the Door
Michael Robinson
2000–2004

The story of this vicious killing starts at a farewell party in Newcastle. The party was thrown in honour of sports student Sara Cameron, who was about to leave for Australia on a work placement from her college at the University of Northumbria. She was excited at the prospect of having some time there, especially as it would coincide with the Sydney Olympics. Sara had her circle of friends, her hopes and ambitions. She was fit and in good health but she was not strong enough to save herself in the shadows of a Newcastle night in April.

The pattern of events leading up to her death is sickeningly familiar. Before midnight, she left the party to go home and, with a small gift in a bag in her hand, took a Metro train to Shiremoor. Her friends at the party were fellow sports students and they had given her a present and a best wishes card. But, on the journey home, Sara caught the eye of a night-time predator, a man with an urge to rape and assault. Possessed with an animal urge to do the worst that night, he followed her when she got off the train and started walking home. Sara only had to walk for half a mile. She never made it.

Michael Robinson, twenty-nine, had meant to catch a train to another suburb earlier that night but had missed it, and somehow this had sealed Sara's fate. As he followed her on the street, a man on crutches came towards him and he had to slow down, but when the man had gone past and he thought he was in the clear, Robinson caught up with Sara and forced her to the ground. She was just a few yards from home when he took her and pulled her into a field close by. There he raped and strangled her. It was heartless and vicious in the extreme.

The attacker attempted to cover his tracks by burning her clothes but some were later found, not too far away from the scene. Her body was found the next day by a man out walking his dog. She was lying under a hedge. The scene has that sickeningly gross and demeaning hue of the sexually motivated killing.

Robinson knew that, as had happened in the Pitchfork case (Chapter 3) a local DNA testing process would begin because the nature of the attack would suggest that the killer knew the immediate terrain. He was right – in addition to 8,000 house-to-house enquiries by police officers, the DNA of over 5,000 men in the area was tested, but it was all to no avail. The police also had what seemed like a useful sighting of a man wearing a distinctive fleece coat on footage from CCTV. In addition, quite a lot of information about the killer had been obtained from the crime scene, including the fact that he was a left-handed smoker. There were plenty of minor details but nothing of great importance in terms of finding a person with a motive and an opportunity.

Detectives on murder cases of this kind hate to let go. The term 'cold case' is a negative, defeatist phrase and officers will say that, when they do have to walk away and leave a case unsolved, it leaves a bad taste in their mouth, and drains confidence and strength. The men on this case did not want that feeling, so they determinedly persisted. A cold case left cold is like turning from a main road into a dark back alley and feeling that there is no reverse.

Three years after her death, the mystery of who had killed Sara was still 'hot' in the police files and it continued to trouble the investigating team. Advances in video technology were able to provide them with more finely tuned imaging and they enlarged the pictures of a man seen crossing the rail track to catch the Earsdon train at the right time for the attack. The terrain was receptive to such a plan of attack: noise, darkness and the cries and laughs of people going home after a night on the drink.

For the police, the community and Sara's family and friends the lack of progress was frustrating. There had been all the usual responses made after such a terrible killing, such as rewards being offered (one local man put up £7,000) and the circulation of her photograph. Sara, who came from Devon, was a very pretty blonde, slim and athletic, and she was aiming to make sport management her career. The too-familiar contrast between that hope and promise and the hard, terrible facts of the way she died is something that can never be explained in the right words.

Even the Ministry of Defence had made a contribution to the police work being done, and it must have seemed as though the case was heading up a dead end when DS Bolam answered the phone and learned that there was a match for the DNA sample that forensics had collected at the scene. As so often in these cases - and this was true even for the Ripper investigation – there was an element of luck. Robinson had landed himself in trouble, this time from some violence in North Shields a year before – he was a man who made trouble wherever he went. When the call came in, Robinson was living down south in Newhaven in Sussex. For the officers involved in such a long investigation, the early morning arrest as Robinson was about to get into his car, must have been very satisfying.

Michael Robinson had indeed been a hell-raiser. He had been responsible for a catalogue of misdemeanours, from stealing car components to using a pepper spray in a fight. These offences took place in locations that were far apart from each other.

Aspects of this man's psychological make-up were beginning to fit the profile of a certain type of serial killer, and the known facts indicate that he may well have killed again. He was a particular kind of drifter with a puzzling work record that involved everything from a spell in the Household Cavalry to casual work and employment once as a coach driver. That he was not considered to be the right type for an army career is particularly telling.

Other traits also fitted the offender profile, as it emerged that he had, at one time, attacked people in his own family and had even killed family pets. Under questioning, he confessed that he had fantasies about committing sexual assaults.

In August 2004 he was in court in Newcastle and the DNA evidence ensured his fate. The pleas relating to murder, rape and GBH were guilty. What could he possibly use as a line of defence? There was the fact that he was drunk, but that is no kind of feature in a case of this kind. In addition, there was his statement that he did not intend to rape and kill at the time he joined the train where Sara was sitting. But the forensic evidence all indicated that there had been a violent and ruthless attack by someone using great strength and determination.

There was little point in the man arguing for his innocence as his movements had been captured on film. The video tapes give a vivid sequence of events in this trail of mayhem and suffering. They show him stepping past a musician, scrambling down one side of the platform and crossing the railway line just after eleven thirty. It is with a shudder of foreboding that we realise that at the time Sara was sitting in the carriage, just minutes away from the place in which her life would be taken from her. The tapes also show that, when he got on the train, he sat around twelve feet from her.

Sentencing Robinson to life, the judge, Mr Justice Henriques, said: 'The last minutes of her life must have been terrifying, painful and humiliating.'

What was the actual incident that had made the DNA sample

match possible? In a fit of bad temper, he had slammed an axe through the door of his neighbour in North Shields. As so often happens, a minute detail was the reason for the ultimate failure of the man's reign of terror on the streets. Peter Sutcliffe had been found by an alert officer doing a traffic enquiry at night. The Yorkshire Ripper had his hammer and the rest of his evil accoutrements with him, and so it was his downfall. In Robinson's case, a violent row with a neighbour proved to be his undoing.

The sequence of events and the source of this psychopath's condition are all too familiar. The lone, socially excluded and dysfunctional male haunts urban pubs and clubs. He is a predator in search of his own brand of perverse and twisted fulfilment. Whether it is a serial killer like Robert Napper and his urge to destroy, as if possessed, or Robinson with the right mental attitude for destruction and inflicting pain on others, brutal crime shows that, for some, it takes very little for such men to kill. DS Bolam stressed that, in this case, it was patience and some luck combined that brought about 'a result'. But the story of Robinson and the pattern of his life are also interesting from the point of view of geographical profiling. Robinson knew the streets around the victim's home very well. He had an instinct for the thoughts and movements of young women at the time and in his home territory. But profiling, as discussed in the previous chapter, is still an inexact science. All we can say here is that the man who cracked an axe through that door in North Shields was a man who had long had sexual fantasies and violent ones, too. He had his 'patch'. He also had the alacrity required of the night killer who knows his topography from previous walks and journeys.

In fact, it would seem highly likely that he knew his victim's place of residence – after passing the man with the crutch, he felt he had to act quickly, surely knowing that Sara's home was just a few feet away. There is a force that ties a killer to a place, and that is as strong as the landscape itself. What we often forget about desperate, amoral killers is that they have thought things through, trying to anticipate anything that might act as a stumbling block or a barrier to what they want. But they cannot think of everything and there is always the element of haste when a small detail or event gets in the way. No matter how careful they are, there is some kind of touch, and every touch leaves a trace. With rapid advances in the technology of DNA testing, identity is not such a special, untouchable thing any more when it comes to the law.

Chapter 15

Still Hope – Sixty-three Years On
1946–2009

Twelve-year-old Muriel Drinkwater got off her school bus at the end of a track leading to her house on 27 June 1946, and started to walk the mile across country to her home at Tyle-Dy farm. It was a track that dipped and rose, and so her mother Margaret could see her in the distance where there was a gap in the trees at one point. They waved to each other, Margaret put the kettle on and waited to welcome her daughter and have a chat about the day. It was an ordinary day: Margaret had been to sell some eggs, and Muriel had been to school, enjoying a sing-song on the school bus coming home. She never arrived home that day and normality simply disappeared into a dark cloud of pain and loss.

Muriel was attacked, raped and killed by that path, and her body was found the day after she had started the walk home, located hidden in a plantation of larch trees. The savagery was staggeringly gross and extreme: she had been shot twice in the chest after being beaten on the head. The killer was careless, throwing the gun into the undergrowth, and that army issue Colt 45 automatic (from the Great War) was later to be sent to the FBI for tests. Unbelievably for an unsolved case, the killer, who had been lying in wait and clearly knew Muriel's movements that day, left a heap of litter where he had been standing: cigarette-ends, sweet papers and bread.

In *The Times* two days later the bare announcement seems to predict the mystery of the business: 'The body of a 12-year-old schoolgirl, Muriel Drinkwater, daughter of a farmer, of Penllergaer, near Swansea, was found yesterday in a wood a quarter of a mile from her home.' The report was placed beside another report of a woman found dead in Newcastle. It reads like just two more everyday attacks on women walking alone; no one could have predicted that over sixty years later, there would be a team of forensic scientists working on the case, but that is what is now happening.

The DNA revolution will at least free people from blame, even if the killer is found and has died. The evidence will achieve several things, but mainly it will exonerate suspects. One of these, arguably the main suspect at the time, is Hubert Hoyles, now seventy-five years old. He was the last person to see Muriel alive, and he was interviewed in November 2008. Hubert was formerly a factory worker but on that fateful day in 1946 he was the person who had bought eggs from Margaret Drinkwater, walking past the girl as she walked home. He said, 'I'd usually see Muriel as she made her way from school and we'd exchange a hello... I saw her that day. She was just minutes from her house when we crossed on the path near the woods where she was killed.' Hubert has been swabbed and exonerated, after all those years – years in which he has had to suffer the feelings that people were talking about him behind his back.

Hubert was just thirteen at the time, and he recalls Muriel as being lovely, and always happy; he told reporters that, 'I've lived with the knowledge that some people in this community suspected me... I knew in the eyes of some people I was the murderer. It blighted my life.' It was noted in the interview with him that over the years he has never spoken of the murder, except to police and a little to his wife; it seems highly likely that Hubert actually passed the probable killer, because he recalls that a few weeks before her death he passed a man in the exact spot where the murder was to be done. He said,

'I'd been up to the farm one afternoon when, at exactly the spot along the route... a smartly dressed man in his thirties suddenly emerged without noise from the bushes.' If that was indeed the killer, then if he were alive today, assuming he was thirty then, he would be ninety-nine years old today. Hubert recalled that, 'There was a menace about him. A wickedness.'

Of course, after the body was found there was a massive and intensive hunt for clues and for any kind of lead that might appear. Hubert himself was taken to a temporary police base, because detectives from the Yard had arrived and they wanted him to look at some potential suspects, based on his report. The man he had seen had spoken to him, so he would know the voice. Hubert had said that the man at the murder location had said, 'What are you doing here?' He had had a local accent and looked 'terribly stern'. He spoke again, telling the boy to get on his way. But the identity parade came up with no lead. The search escalated.

There were 3,000 mourners at Muriel's funeral at St David's church at Penllergaer; recently a new headstone was placed there, paid for by the local Girl Guide troop. The farmland has now gone, and Muriel's parents, last heard of in Cheshire, and her sisters, are believed to be dead.

Police went to ask questions at every farmhouse and home in a range of 150 miles from the murder scene; they even spoke to men in Swansea and in rural areas as far away as Carmarthenshire. Chief Inspector Paul Bethell spoke to the *Daily Mail* about the matter, and said that in 2005, he came across Muriel's clothing in an old store cupboard, and the case was to be 'hot' again. There they were, coat, underwear and school uniform, and there was a yellow circle marked on her coat, surrounding a semen stain. As Bethell said, 'There are people who have lived with the finger of blame pointing at them for years and at last we have the scientific technology to say it wasn't him...'

Before the announcement that there was to be a DNA

testing of that stain, there had already been theories and suspects in the press. One writer, Neil Milkins, has said that the killer was Harold Jones, a man who killed two young girls in Abertillery in the 1920s. Jones was out of prison in 1946, and Milkins sees startling similarities between the two cases. He wrote a book on his theories, *Every Mother's Nightmare*, and in that he says that 'People around here have always told tales about Harold Jones and the terrible things he did, so I decided to find out the truth.' Jones disappeared into obscurity after being released from Wandsworth prison in 1941, and he had escaped the noose only because of his age, but had confessed to the killing of little Freda Burnell while in prison in Usk. Milkins notes that Jones would visit his parents in Rhiw Parc Road 'and the sound of him playing the organ in their front room would haunt the terraced streets, all of which would be empty as mothers kept their children safe indoors until he'd gone away again.'

If this is the killer, then we may be talking about the notorious 'Jack the Stripper' – if Milkins is right, then Jones, who was only fifteen when he killed Burnell and another girl, was on the loose for twenty years before the 'Stripper' murders in Hammersmith in the years 1964-65. This unknown serial killer copied Jack the Ripper, and he killed six prostitutes whose nude bodies were thrown into the Thames. After CS John Du Rose of the Yard led the case investigation and interviewed 7,000 men in connection with the murders, he gave out the wrong information that there were just twenty suspects, then eventually he announced that there were only three men in the frame, and the killings stopped. Did he move to South Wales and was he the Harold Jones that Milkins argues? There was one main suspect, but he took his own life. After that, the craziest suggestions have been put forward, but Milkins' reasoning is sound. It would be truly amazing if the DNA matched the Jones family. Harold Jones died in Hammersmith in 1971, and if he was Jack the Stripper, then a cold case which has no link to DNA research will be sorted out. If indeed he was the killer of Muriel Drinkwater, then all we have to go on in terms of material from the time is the report from the young boy at the time, Hubert Hoyles.

We also have the statements made by Diane Lazarus, the psychic consultant. A few years ago, Diane worked on the Drinkwater case, and she gave an account of the girl's walk home from the bus, her being raped, and being attacked by someone she knew well, 'a friend' as Diane says. An old man living in the area was identified by Diane's investigation, and of course, the results of the DNA work will perhaps validate that account. This is not an example of sheer desperation, as a more cynical view of the place of psychic insights in detective work might say; on the contrary, there has been plenty of evidence in many parts of the world in recent years to make police forces consider the potentially perceptive and amazingly accurate narratives provided by psychics. Diane Lazarus certainly gave an account that fell in line with a number of features not generally known.

It may well be that Harold Jones was the stern man on the path that day. His psychopathic profile actually suggests that he was schizophrenic. It could be that Y-STR (short tandem repeat, relating to the male, Y chromosome) testing (on male descendants) may yet be possible, but in the interim, the work being done on the stain on Muriel's clothing is under the supervision of Dr Colin Dark in Cambridge. Dr Dark explained what was done to find the semen traces to the *Daily Mail*: 'The test we use is the same test that would have been used at the time... you take a swab, moisten a piece of filter paper, touch the swab against it, then spray the filter paper with a coloured chemical. There is a chemical inside semen that will change the colour from brown to purple.' After that, with a positive result, the sample was dissolved in a liquid chemical and the specimen was then put on a slide, under a microscope. This showed that sperm was there.

The next step is to apply the Y-DNA and Dr Dark is still developing this. This looks at the repeat sequences on the profile that are from the male line; this shadows the same type of profile as the mitochondrial DNA, as discussed in Chapter 2. The coding genes are found within the short arm of the Y chromosome, and these create the determination of sex; in more current cases of sexual assault, a vaginal swab will contain both male and female DNA and up to the present it has been difficult to study the male component, because both the male and female components tend to be amplified and not completely separated. Dr Dark is working on this, so that the Y-DNA in the sample from Muriel's coat will be subject to study and definition. If the Y-STR is examined and isolated, there will be no masking effect of the profile.

The police work from the first stage of the inquiry is now being repeated by CI Bethell, who has said that there will be around fifty men, all local to the area, who need to be swabbed, for the same exoneration as that for Hubert Hoyles. It has to be said that when the DNA matching is finally complete, it will probably be the case that sons or grandsons will become aware that their father or grandfather was the killer of little Muriel. It will be recalled that in the Lynette White case (Chapter 6) it was familial DNA that led to the arrest of Gafoor. The increasing knowledge about familial DNA is bringing apparent revisions to a number of crimes in Britain – and almost daily.

Clearly, this case raises questions about the reasons for such distantly 'cold' cases. Some would argue that such re-investigations mean that vast sums of money and staff time will be spent with no tangible return on that investment. But a cold case is more than a file left to gather dust. Muriel Drinkwater's clothes were found in that cupboard, just as found on the day of her death. That means somehow the moment frozen in time was a moment of pain and terror. There may not be retribution available but there is closure possible now. It is impossible to avoid the sense of stigma that may attach to descendants of the killer when known, but that has no substance anyway; a far more positive conclusion is to reflect that there will be justice, however late arriving, and there will be a number of men who will have a sense of freedom given to them after decades under a cloud of vague but still worrying suspicion.

In one sense, the very fact that the coat was still there in the cupboard, with the yellow circle around the stain, and that the stain was semen from the killer, is close to miraculous, and it is to be hoped that this case is not the only one in this collection of stories, with the exception of Oetzi, that remains cold. It would be a cruel twist of fate to reflect that a murder of sixty-three years ago would stay as cold as the identity of the Alpine killer from 3,000 BC. Next day's newspaper headlines could bring the news that everyone CI Bethell and plenty of other people in South Wales are waiting for, and when it does, it will be arguably the most stunning triumph for Dr Dark and the forensic team in their history.

Chapter 16

Peter Tobin
1991–2009

There were many who thought, in September, 2006, that a fourteen-year sentence should be a fourteen-year sentence – not a ten-year sentence. That was because handyman Peter Tobin, working in St Patrick's Roman Catholic Church in Anderston, Glasgow, murdered student Angelika Kluk. He had been released in 2004, after being sentenced to do fourteen years at Winchester Crown Court for attacking two teenage girls who were babysitting his son in Havant. He assaulted and raped them at knifepoint and then took off into what he thought was anonymity, but the crime was featured on Crimewatch and he was tracked down. If he had been in gaol, the public would have been safe for a little longer and Angelika would have lived.

But we are dealing with a relentlessly predatory serial killer here, who is now in gaol for life but who has probably killed many more women than the current record shows. The way he ruthlessly murdered and buried Angelika typified the amoral rapacity of the man: he met her because she was working as a cleaner at the church, to earn money to help studies back home in Gdansk. She was attacked in a garage, beaten and raped, and then buried – but it is believed that she was still alive when he put her in an underground chamber. The killing took place probably on 24 September 2006, and he was arrested just after her body was found on the 29th of that month. This was to be just the beginning of a series of investigations, and the case has become one of the most stunning of all the achievements of DNA in forensics. The trial for Angelika's murder lasted for six weeks, being held at the High Court of Justiciary, Edinburgh, in 2007. Tobin was found guilty of the murder and given a life sentence, to serve at least twenty-one years. Lord Menzies referred to him as 'an evil man'. Later events in the opening of some cold cases was certainly to prove that.

As Tobin was in gaol, Strathclyde detectives began to suspect a link between Tobin and some murders elsewhere, notably the disappearance of Vicky Hamilton because Tobin had been living in Bathgate at the time fifteen-year-old Vicky disappeared. Bert Swanson, of the Lothian and Borders force, was then the cold case review manager, and he initiated what was to be called Operation Mahogany. There was an obvious first step for Swanson – to have a purse looked at. This had been Vicky's purse and had been found in Bathgate, in the road near the bus station; it had always seemed that her attacker had left the purse there for police to find, so that it would be assumed that she had left town and run away from home for some reason.

The DNA on the purse proved to be a match to that of Tobin's son, Daniel. Swanson said that at that point the cold case inquiry took off and moved quickly towards a search of Tobin's known address down south, in Margate. In November 2007, a search at that place, an ordinary semi where neighbours remembered Tobin well, led to the discovery of Vicky's body. She had been cut in two and parts of her body put in bin bags. But regarding the DNA match with Tobin, the best news for Swanson was that police found a knife at that address, and there was Vicky's DNA on it; they could compare that with records at Yorkhill Hospital in Glasgow, because her blood had been stored there after a Guthrie test had been taken. This is a heel-prick test that is routinely carried out on new-born babies.

In the search at Margate, first radar had detected an anomaly in the soil; forensic archaeologists were working before there was

DNA analysis of course. When the plastic bags were then found after the dig, Tobin's fingerprints were on them. It was to emerge in court that Tobin had worked on digging for the placements of the mains for the Brighton Water Board back in the 1970s, and he was a very skilled digger. In fact, when this was pointed out, and Vicky's body in the soil described, there was a palpably emotional reaction in court. Not only was there the discovery of the prints, but also Tobin's DNA was on Vicky's body and, as it was known that he drugged his victims.

The girl who had been staying with her sister back in 1991, and had then started her journey home, even from the grave provided evidence that would convict her killer. Vicki gave her sister a hug that night in February, and waited for her bus in the centre of Livingston. She had phoned her father but he had not been at home; we know that she went to buy some fish and chips and that she asked there about the next bus. Keith Anderson, the officer who was in charge of the case at the time, commented: 'Hanging around in the centre of Bathgate that evening was a seedy former council-worker turned car mechanic, whose name was Peter Tobin.' Vicky, wearing a black bomber jacket and jeans, and some borrowed jewellery, was a vulnerable target for this predator on the loose.

What happened after that is largely conjecture. He most likely took her to his house at Robertson Avenue. There he very likely promised to take her home, and it is known now that he gave her a drug, amitryptiline, which is an anti-depressant: a large dose would have been a very strong sedative. This was found in her liver at the Margate dig. Tobin then, as is surmised after forensic tests, pressed her onto the floor and sodomised her after hitting her and grabbing her by the neck; there was evidence to show that she had tried to fight. Tobin apparently went for a drink after that, because he was seen at around half past ten and he had shouted out to a neighbour.

Vicky's corpse was then dismembered and she was wrapped and packaged; his son, Daniel, then came to stay with him and it was at that point that he must have given the boy Vicky's purse to play with, and the boy's saliva was on the purse – hence the tracing of the DNA later. Daniel was living with his mother in Portsmouth, and was taken back home; then Tobin must have left for Margate. There is a record of him being treated in hospital at this time – with pains in his stomach. We can only guess what the cause of that might have been. But he was soon down south and by March, 1991 he was living at 50 Irvine Drive, Margate. After that, as he was a chatty man who was skilled at spinning yarns, he responded to a neighbour's questions about his digging in the garden by saying he was making a sandpit for the kid when he visited. He did indeed make a sandpit, and even made a cement surface for the packages beneath the sand.

A neighbour, David Martin, testified, and gave some remarkably helpful and perceptive comments: 'The first thing you realise about Peter Tobin is how normal he is. He's not something that crawls out of the woodwork even if that's what appears at a later stage. No, he's absolutely normal – like talking to your best mate or someone down the pub.' Mr Martin had actually seen the grave being dug and was told it was the sandpit. He recalled joking with Tobin that he was planning to dig 'to Australia'. Tobin then told the story of the sandpit.

But there was something else, and this suggests the depth of Tobin's iniquity: another body was found at the Margate house. This proved to be Dinah McNicol, eighteen, who had been missing since 1991. After finding Vicky, police had lifted up the whole of the patio there. Dinah, it is known, took a lift from a stranger after going to a music festival in Hampshire. No other bodies were later found there. Tobin had not lived there long, but it is now apparent that wherever he lived in his rather nomadic life, there tends to be evidence of his repulsive psychopathic life. Since his 1994 conviction for rape, buggery and indecent assault, it has become clear that several other attacks have his imprint in that respect, and that Kluk, Hamilton and McNicol may be just some of many more victims as yet unknown.

Regarding the DNA evidence: it was stated that the chance of the DNA found on the knife in Margate being from someone other than Vicky was more than a billion to one. Swabs taken from her body also showed some of the DNA from Tobin, and this suggested the pattern of his sexual tastes when he attacked – sodomising victims. The scientist who gave evidence in court, Nicola Clayson, explained that DNA from intimate locations on Vicky matched seven out of twenty numbers on Tobin's profile, so the recurrence ratio was 1 in 34,000 and an external swab matched four out of twenty. The probability ratios in these instances were low – 1 in 114 for the latter. Naturally, the defence challenged this, but Ms Clayson explained: 'The DNA profile that we obtained cannot be specifically assigned with 100 per cent certainty to any particular body fluid.' Naturally, the defence pointed out that 1 in 114 meant that of all people in Scotland, 428,571 could have that profile. It was a partial one, due to the degraded material. But there was no denying the evidence with regard to the knife.

When asked how the skin got on the knife and how the knife got in the loft where it was found, Tobin simply said, 'I haven't got a clue but it was my knife that was in the loft. End of story.'

After some tissue was taken from a knife found in the Bathgate house, a virtually full match was found with Vicky's DNA. It was also confirmed at the trial that the DNA on the purse was from Tobin's son, whom he saw only at weekends. When pressed on aspects of his life and movements at the time of the murder, all Tobin could say was, 'Just back and forward… but if it was the weekend I would have had the wee one with me anyway.' He was trying to imply that he was incapable of any such crime when in charge of his son. But the boy's DNA on the purse made a mockery of that.

When Tobin was sentenced, there was a shout of 'Yes' in court and as he was handcuffed and taken down to the court cell, there were cries of 'Rot in Hell' and 'Goodbye from Vicky's dad!' One of the most touching aspects of the trial, after such a long time of uncertainty and pain on the part of the victims' families, was that Vicky's sister, who mentioned Angelika Kluk, saying, 'We would like to take the opportunity to offer our condolences to the family and friends of Angelika Kluk... We know only too well the hurt and grief they will have suffered.'

On the night of her death, Vicky had come across Tobin and she had trusted him. When a chef found Vicky's purse, just eleven days after she had gone missing, it was to be the start of a long journey towards truth – a brutal truth that resonates still. However, as with most of these cases in which the forces of law have to cope with a trail of victims and lives in disarray in the aftermath of murder, new openings have come along. One of the most notable of these, featured in detail in the *Sunday Mail* in December 2008, concerns Jessie Earl. Profiler David Wilson is researching Tobin's criminal career and we will no doubt learn much more about this man, born in Paisley in 1946, the youngest of eight. We might learn that he was also the killer of Jessie, who disappeared twenty-eight years ago, and whose remains were found in a thicket on Beachy Head not long after an appeal on a chat show in which Terry Wogan talked to the parents.

Her parents were interviewed in the *Sunday Mail* in the light of Tobin's conviction, and Wilson added some of his thoughts as a profiler to that sad story. Jessie was a second-year student at Eastbourne College of Art and Design. She called her mother from a phone box at the sea front to say that she would be going home to them in London, but she never made it. Tobin was living twenty-five miles away at the time. Jessie's mother went down to Eastbourne and sensed that there was something wrong. Jessie had been seen by many people up to a certain time, and then nothing. There was a massive, widespread search for her, including police helicopters over the coast and an intensive missing persons campaign. Her father, John, told the press after his daughter's remains were found: 'He [a man flying a kite] saw the skull first, then found the rest of the bones. It must have been terrible for him... When we were told the remains were Jessie's my immediate feeling was relief. I knew I should be shocked but I wasn't. It was like a weight had been lifted from us.'

No doubt the string of potential further victims of Tobin will lead on to all kinds of possible crimes, and perhaps the most momentous of these will answer the question of whether or not Tobin is the same person as the notorious 'Bible John'. Bible John is the name given to a killer who was active in the 1960s in the dance halls of Glasgow, notably the Barrowlands. The context was one of courting and relaxing, noise, drink and sexual approaches; but there were three murders of women within a three-month period. It has almost entered the realm of folklore rather than of crime history now. There are some features in common with Bible John and Tobin: he was living in Glasgow in 1968-69, and physical descriptions tally quite well. The victims had all been dancing in Barrowlands, all were strangled and the killer earned his nickname because of his religious remarks and moral views. Tobin was indeed a Roman Catholic (hence his job at the church when he met and killed Kluk); he was just twenty-one at the time of the first killing, and a photofit of Bible John could well match a younger-looking Tobin.

Police have never given up hope of nailing 'Bible John' and the search goes on. In 1996, a former soldier, John McInnes, took his own life, and he had been a suspect; but DNA analysis has cleared him. There have been other candidates, including a name given to psychologist Ian Stephen in 2000, but that has not developed into anything definite. Could Peter Tobin be the man? If he was Bible John, he would undoubtedly keep quiet anyway; when detectives went to see him in gaol with regard to locating Vicky's body, before the Margate connection, their pleas came to nothing. A *Times* reporter explained: 'When the detectives shuffled their papers together and prepared to rise from their seats, they appealed to the scruffy convict one more time… would he now, for the sake of the family, tell them where the body was? His reply was, 'Sorry, I cannae help you…'

If Tobin and Bible John are one and the same person, maybe profiler David Wilson will help to sort out the motivations; he told reporters, with regard to Tobin's modus operandi:

'I believe there are many more victims… this is not the behaviour of a man who was killing for the first time –by the time he killed Vicky he had in all likelihood already perfected the way that he killed and developed a very acute sense of what he wanted to achieve by the death of his victim.' When he explained this, Wilson said, 'By achieve I mean what purpose this death meant to him: was it sexual, or symbolic or perhaps both.' If there is a case for defining Tobin as Bible John, the answer might lie in DNA eventually. But at the moment, the experts in deviant psychology are opening up more speculations.

Chapter 17

Trapped after Returning a Knife
Steven Sellars
1996–2007

S ometimes a sense of injustice, or even wanting to make a fuss about someone's mistake, can open up a can of worms. This is exactly what happened in the Steven Sellars story. In 2007, Sellars, then forty-one and a family man, walked into York High School brandishing a Stanley knife. This is the standard knife for all kinds of craft skills of course, and it was used in headmaster, Mr Ellis's, school. This trip to school to make a point about health and safety, was to lead to prison for Sellars.

Sellars' son Liam had brought the knife home from school and his father was outraged. A report on this, before there was any question of Sellars the criminal, noted that he had come across as a well-meaning and responsible citizen, 'doing the right thing': 'I offered to take the knife back, as any responsible parent would do, on my way to the doctor's to pick up a prescription.' He seemed to want sympathy at that point from press and public, and continued, 'I spoke to the receptionist, who at no time appeared distressed. I told her the reason I was there and showed her the knife discreetly. I then immediately put it in my pocket.'

Any parent would be concerned if a knife was brought home from school, and Sellars spoke to the Head. Apparently there had not been a shadow board used in class, or there would not have been a response as claimed by Sellars that the Head admitted that he had no knowledge of how many of the knives might be missing. The outraged Sellars withdrew his son from the school until an apology was given. But to aggravate the situation, the Head had called police – after all a man had entered his school carrying knife. When this was first reported, it appeared to be the kind of story the newspapers love – a criticism of the beleaguered education system. Sellars said, 'There was absolutely no need for matters to be taken to the extremes they were... if any complaint had been dealt with professionally from the start none of this would have happened.' How right he was, but also how ironical that he should be detained and a swab taken, even though he was at the time released without charge. He had been about to phone home when two officers arrived and arrested him.

It has to be said, with regard to the ongoing civil liberties debate about DNA records on the national database and the swabbing of people without a charge made, that in this case a rapist was caught by that DNA test. This is because Steven Sellars had attempted to rape a York student back in 1996. The man who said he was 'arrested for doing the right thing, for telling the truth and being honest' was a man with form. In April 1996, he had attacked the nineteen-year-old student as she walked home, forced her to the ground and punched her, but her calls for help brought people to the scene and Sellars had run off. The victim said at the time, 'I want this man to be caught, and I don't want him out there to do it to somebody else. I'm angry he thinks he's got away with it.' In the attack, Sellars had threatened her with the words: 'Keep quiet and I won't kill you!'

He had also previously committed rape in South Yorkshire in 1989, and another in Leeds in 1993. When he was investigated and his computer searched, it was revealed that he had made internet searches for 'rape fantasy' and other related subjects. The swab taken after his righteous complaint had been the net that trapped him. The first newspaper report lays on his earnestness with a style of overkill, down to his statement that he never intended to scare anyone, saying that 'The farce which followed just proved to me what a joke the education system is.' He told the press that the knife had been returned to 'its incompetent owners'.

Naturally, as this was reported in the context of Mail OnLine, there were sympathetic responses from the public, such as, 'With this and many other reports of stupid policing many will wonder what purpose many officers serve...' That has to be the most ironical statement in the case. Shortly after this well-meaning but distorted account of the knife complaint, Steven Sellars was in court at York. In early December, this serial sex-attacker started a life sentence. The prosecutor at the trial described how Sellars in 1996 had grabbed the student then 'placed his hand over her mouth to stop her screaming... She was terrified.'

That student had bitten his finger, and there was the source of the DNA that was to trap him all those years later. Despite his previous convictions, the national DNA database was very new then and his DNA was not on that source for a match to be made. But of course, the DNA was retained and after the fiasco at the High School, then a match was made to the 1996 attack. Sellars had been given three previous gaol sentences, and it emerged that his sex crimes began with indecent assaults on two eleven-year-old girls.

The public who criticised the police and who applauded his good work in returning the craft knife now reviled him; he was jeered by the families and friends of his victim as he was taken down. Judge Stephen Ashurst, presiding, summed up by saying that Sellars targeted and waited for a lone woman and attacked her; the judge said, 'You threatened her and she feared she was going to be killed. I have to bear in mind that for the last twelve years your victim has had to wonder if her attacker is still at large and if he will ever face justice. You have devastated her life.'

It came as something of a surprise that Sellars would be able to apply for parole after four years. In prison, if he attends a sex offender treatment programme and insists on having looked objectively at his sexual deviance and his violence, the application could be made, and it has to be asked, with many previous cases in this book in mind, just how much we now understand that 'career trajectory' of the serious sex offender and whether that sickness of mind is treatable or curable. The pattern shows, in case after case, that in these categories of offence, step one is voyeurism and masturbatory fantasy, while the last stage in that dangerous road is a shift from private to public, and someone is attacked, raped and often murdered. As the judge said, Sellars is 'a complex, unpredictable and dangerous man' and whose remorse was 'shallow and contrived'.

That is what the criminal justice system is up against in these cases: the dilemma that remorse could equal either a convincing acting performance or a genuine and profound sense of shame that brings about a change in a man's life. The related factors, discussed in previous chapters, of crime mapping and profiling have something of a template here: the 1996 attack was done near the University Science Park: in university areas of cities, there is a distinct community with its own habits, routines, and indeed geographical features. People may come and go at almost all times, and students may brush shoulders with non-students. In other words, although there is vigilance on campuses, of course, maybe the time has come for the profilers to apply ideas to this, and to relate that to practical policing. It was noted in one report on Sellars that a year earlier in York there had been a rape by a student on a fellow student – and this was a man with previous convictions.

It could be that the DNA database needs to be parallel to a series of geographical crime mapping records, and that is what is increasingly being done. It would not necessarily pre-empt the kind of crime committed by Sellars and others, but it would give the police a chance to apply some preventive action. Meanwhile, the York students can live without the fear that there is a dangerous man loitering around the campus. Sellars can brood on his egoistic display of a 'wrong' and how his righteous indignation led him a step too far – to a prison cell.

Chapter 18

Closing in: The Death of Colette Aram 1983–present

would like this chapter to be my one small contribution to the justice this sad death deserves. DNA science has brought police to this killer, but the more there is in print about this savage, meaningless death of a child, the more chance there will be of retribution and a sense of a wound healing, if wounds in the heart can ever heal.

Sometimes, writing murder casebook stories can be an appeal for closure on many levels: but at the heart of this kind of narrative is a desire for the trauma to be erased. When a child dies in violent circumstances, there is undoubtedly another dimension of personal suffering in the relatives, and this seeps through all the media reports and the sometimes unhealthy interest in the circumstances of the case. That was so with Lesley Molseed in particular, and is arguably just as poignant in this case. The murder of Colette Aram in 1983 led to such prominent appeals and statements regarding her mother in particular that it has been impossible for anyone interested in forensics and the potential justice that science might hold to remain totally objective.

With this case that situation is even more prominent because it was the first appeal broadcast on the *Timewatch* programme on Thursday 7 June 1984. Incredibly for a case with so many sightings and descriptions of the likely killer, *Timewatch* broadcast the story again twenty-five year later. In 2008, her mother, Jacqui Kirkby, held an interview with police on that twenty-fifth anniversary, saying, 'I was sitting in an armchair by the window... there was a police officer by the front door and one at the top of the drive, and as my son and stepfather came back I just saw them shake their heads and I knew straightaway.' Her reaction was a real paradox, in line with how we deal with a death close to us: first she screamed and then phoned work, calmly to say that she would not be at work because her daughter had been murdered. For days afterwards all she could do was sit behind closed curtains because Jacqui notes that the family were made to feel like 'some kind of tourist attraction'.

The body of Colette was found on 31 October 1983 in a field not far from where she lived in Keyworth, Nottinghamshire. She had been attacked savagely and killed in a frenzy: strangled and raped. She was seen by her brother Mark, who came across the scene after her naked body had been found by police. Colette had been walking to her boyfriend's house. Her killer had been seen by all kinds of people and he appears not to have worried too much about being seen, maybe even visiting a pub in such a way that it seems like a very amateurish attempt to create an alibi.

A man went to the *Generous Britain* pub in Costock nearby, and was seen drinking an orange juice and lemonade. He was described as being white, between twenty-five and thirty-five, and tall with dark wavy hair, having a broad nose and of medium build. He talked to the landlady and it was remembered that he ate a ham and ploughman's cob. The fact that he spoke to the landlady and told a story (which made no sense to her) makes this seem like a ploy to make an alibi. Even more telling was the detail that blood was noticed on his hand.

Throughout the day, there had been a series of reports, beginning with several sightings of a red Ford Fiesta that was later known to have been stolen. This was seen parked outside a house at Mount Pleasant at a quarter to five, then a teenage girl was followed in such a car, seen at 6.20 and again at 6.40. The man was desperate for a victim, as he almost certainly approached another young girl as she was walking her dog. A little later – and this is the most convincing evidence that this was the killer – a man was seen in a parked red Fiesta, and he had a knife. It was later discovered that the car had been stolen in West Bridgford.

It was around eight o'clock when Colette set off for her boyfriend's house, and at ten past eight screams were heard on Nicker Hill, exactly where Colette had walked, and she was last seen alive by some friends who walked past her. The Fiesta was found by police the next day, again parked in the street in Mount Pleasant. The scenario reads like the kind of actions a predatory killer with a definite type of prey would have had in mind: he wanted someone young, pretty and far from strong enough to fight back. It seems certain that she was first abducted because people heard screams and the sound of a car door being slammed. Her body was found half a mile away, close to a known 'lovers lane'.

There was an intensive police operation, of course. In fact, it was the most determined and widespread investigation ever conducted in the county. Five weeks after the murder, the police received a letter, in the manner of the infamous 'Yorkshire Ripper' letter, supposed to be written by the killer. In that note he said that he had been wearing a Halloween mask, but that was not confirmed.

After twenty years, there was another broadcast appeal; DS Chris Barnfather told the press that there had been an overwhelming response to the call for information. He said, 'We've had calls from prison officers in high security units … from police officers up and down the country, handwriting experts, ex-prisoners, members of the public generally, from Scotland to the Channel Islands.' There had been some local callers too, but Barnfather pointed out that people will not easily give information unless there was a call from the police, knocking on their door. He commented that he wanted the publicity at that time to be like 'the police knocking on their door'.

Then, in October 2008, came the announcement that DNA work had provided a cause for some hope in the case. A DNA profile was recovered in 2007 and work had begun on that. DS Kevin Flint said that the police had 'forensic opportunities' and that they had a DNA profile. The elimination process then began. DS Flint said, 'People will have their suspicions but we have not had the right name.' In fact, there have been eliminations: 1,500 people have been counted out, and also another 800 swabs from local people have been taken. The new campaign is certainly determined: 15,000 newsletters in the area on greatest investigative interest have been distributed.

Meanwhile, the emotional debris in the lives of Colette's relatives is still there: the shattered lives apparent. She was a lively, attractive girl; she just left her school and wanted to walk to see her boyfriend. She was offered a lift by her mum but refused, saying, 'No, I'll be fine. I'll walk.' Jacqui recalls that she gave her daughter a goodbye kiss. She says that her daughter was 'a fun child, always happy, always laughing... I try to imagine all the time what she would be like now, especially when I see girls she was with at school with their families and children.' The *Daily Telegraph* reported, in October 2008, that Jacqui had moved to Greece 'to start a new life'. We have to feel that her appeal at that time may well be the last, and it has all the features of so many such statements, sickeningly familiar to television viewers: 'Please come forward, give the reasons why. Let's have some sort of justice on this for Colette's sake, for her, not for me, not for Mark, not for my ex-husband.'

As with the high-profile case of Brady the Moors Murderer, it is now a familiar pattern: the emotional appeal (or even an appeal with some logic) creates the opposite of pity or empathy with the killer – it makes the offender in question feel a sense of power. The images of searches on Saddleworth Moor after supposed 'information' from Brady or Hindley in prison became powerful symbols of desperation and inverted power, seen on the television screens over the years since those murders in the 1960s.

On 8 April 2009 Paul Stewart Hutchinson was charged with Colette's murder. He has been in the dock at Nottingham Crown Court and now awaits sentence.

There is one coda to the story, and that includes the name Robert Black. He is currently in gaol for life, after a series of killings potentially ranging from 1969 to 1990. A meeting was held in Newcastle in 1994 to consider his implication in eight unsolved cases of murder or disappearance. The victims in this context were killed or disappeared in locations from Devon to Nottingham, and Colette's case was in that group. But no conclusions were reached. But the communication with Black goes on: in April 2008, Black was interviewed in relation to a murder in Ireland in 1981, and he is possibly to be taken back to the murder scene. Black's modus operandi is in line with the circumstances of Colette's death, but of course, his DNA has not matched the profile.

This attempt to check on Black, before the DNA profile was available, makes a powerful illustration of the frustrating limits of serious crime investigation before that forensic advance was made, and in fact in the first years of its use after the Narborough (Pitchfork) case. The focus of investigation has always been the modus operandi and its links to either fundamental principles of detective work or of offender profiling. In the end, all this good work and sheer instinct comes up against the brick wall of the perverse will for power in the psychopath under questioning or investigation.

DNA, above all other achievements, has reduced the necessity of that kind of desperation. As for the Arams, they must have a kind of closure.

Chapter 19

The Shoe Rapist
1983–2006

etishism is recognised as a defined mental illness. It has a known trajectory of behaviour and symptoms. The general agreement is that the person with this illness attaches meanings and emotional responses to inanimate objects. The value of this to the person involved is that the object gives sexual or even physical stimulation. The expression of this may be completely harmless, but it may also be part of the lifestyle and personality composition of a serious sexual offender. This is the story of one such criminal.

The pattern of development in treatment, if the person is under medical supervision, tends to be at least six months of intense sexual stimulation, with related fantasies, linked to desired objects. After that, noticeable impairment in work or relationships will emerge, and there will be limited functioning at home or in the workplace. In this spectrum of stimulus objects, items of clothing are common as stimulants. In this story it is women's shoes which form the causal focus for the man's deviance.

The problem is that the offender at the centre of this story was not under treatment, but studies and case work indicate that such fetishists indulge in such fantasy and attachment because the larger elements of their lives are in many ways affected by inadequacy, doubts on masculinity and stresses in personal relationships. But in the subject of this chapter we have the tale of a dangerous man, prowling for victims – the same man who stood in the dock at Sheffield Crown Court in July 2006, with short, neat hair and wearing a dark suit, black tie and white shirt. He was a company manager and a person thought by many to be 'a pillar of the community'. Sexual fetishism means a dual life, and this hidden nature of the person with the mental illness means a Jekyll and Hyde existence.

One of the most extreme versions of this was in Yokohama, Japan, in 2006. Katsyo Miyake had a visit from the police at his apartment; they found 2,500 pairs of women's panties there, stolen over a ten-year period. Panties were strewn in all areas of his living space, and there seemed to be a special place, under his mattress, in which items of especial significance were kept. Like the man in this story in England, Miyake was a collector, with his own tastes, storage habits and uses for the trophies. He was arrested and is now the subject of a skilled psychiatrist.

Fetishism as a sexual culture has been defined and described since the concept was created by Alfred Binet in 1887, then it was further studied and explained by Richard Krafft-Ebing in 1912. He wrote about the 'animation of body parts'. Of all the varieties of fetishists, the objective one is arguably potentially the commonest criminal type. The man in Sheffield Crown Court needed shoes, and his store was found behind a trapdoor at the printing works where he worked: there were over a hundred pairs of stiletto shoes there. Generally, such fetishistic trophies define the unattainable. But for this man, James Lloyd, who was forty-nine when arrested, the desire was far from that – he 'obtained' by stalking, attacking and raping several women in South Yorkshire between 1983 and 1986.

The victims were young women in their twenties; after the attacks, he would take shoes, and also jewellery from the women. He had struck at Goldthorpe near Barnsley, Rotherham, Hoyland, and in Swinton. There were also shoe thefts and attempted rapes in the string of charges. One victim spoke to the *Daily Mail* in 2006. She recalled that he wore a mask; she said that she was walking home from the pub one night when she was attacked from behind and a knife was pressed to her face. She was then tied up and raped. Her life was ruined by the experience, and her marriage failed. She said, after he was sentenced to life inside, 'Seeing Lloyd arrested and facing a life sentence has helped me to finally feel at rest... I'm satisfied that he has got his just deserts at last.'

Lloyd was a Freemason, and although he was a successful man, with a wife, family and large house, he will always be labelled 'The Shoe Rapist' in the chronicle of modern crimes in Britain. His reign of terror involved walking the streets with stockings and tights for masks and ligatures; that day at Dearne Valley Printers, the game was up and his criminal fetish obsessions at an end, and open to investigation. The good husband had been leading a shadow life, and maintaining the pretence for several years. He was also spoken of as 'Mr Ordinary' – a seeming workaholic who was earning very good money and even working often at weekends; as his fetishistic cache of trophies was in the workplace, this makes total sense, with the wisdom of hindsight, of course.

His crimes were done while he was working as a part-time taxi driver, in the first years of his life with his second wife, whom he married in August 1985. He had been married before, to his childhood sweetheart, and after having a child, they divorced. At that time, the sexual deviance went as far as making sex videos featuring himself and his wife, and it was alleged that his wife was drugged in that particular activity. She later spoke about the whole sorry business, saying, 'I can't relate the husband I know to the man who committed these crimes. I have never had any inkling he had any capacity for anything like this. It is not the person I know and have lived with for all these years.'

In the early stages of the investigation, the crimes were featured on *Crimewatch* and in 2002 the whole case was reviewed; there were 350 names given by callers, but enquiries came to nothing. Lloyd perhaps thought that, as he had probably stopped the crimes after 1986, he would not be traced, but then along came the DNA profiling. As with the Cardiff case of Jeffrey Gafoor, it was mitochondrial DNA matching that caught him. The related tests after his arrest brought up forty-three people with links to the 'Shoe Rapist'. As the police started calling on these individuals, they reached Lloyd's sister, who had a minor motoring offence: her details meant that they had their man. She rang Lloyd to tell him he would have police coming to him, and his first thought was to think of his children, so he asked his father to do that; then he set about taking his own life.

It is impossible to imagine the trauma associated with the son's experience when he found his father in the process of hanging himself, but that is what happened. It does not require a professional psychiatrist to understand how the crimes here implode into the family emotional fabric: the victims are at home as well as on the South Yorkshire streets. The behaviour recorded by Lloyd at that time, before capture, indicates the extreme narcissistic nature of this category of sex offender: everything linked to the material of that personal fantasy, when shredded by the end of the restless terror, ruined everyone with him.

In the Sheffield Crown Court in July 2006, the Recorder of the city, Alan Goldsack QC, gave Lloyd an indeterminate sentence and specified at the very least, fifteen years in prison. He said, 'Few sexual cases are more serious than these... for the last twenty-plus years you have been living a lie, with your family, your friends, your work colleagues, and generally. These were the sort of rapes that are every woman's nightmare. They are terrifying offences, set upon by a stranger whilst walking home, with no help available and not knowing whether the assault will end with sexual degradation or go further.' A statement was also read by the families of the victims, stating, 'We are relieved that this cannot happen to any other women... He has hidden behind the façade of respectability and has shown no remorse for the crimes he has committed.'

The DNA factor in this case was a perfectly straightforward use of the NDNAD (National DNA Database) – relating the driving offence swab record to Lloyd's by the mitochondrial sample. It was a very strong argument in favour of the virtues of the NDNAD, and Detective Sue Hickman was the officer who knocked on Lloyd's sister's door. Hickman recalled that she asked the woman if she had any brothers and the reply was, 'Yes, I've got a brother. But it wouldn't be my brother. He's a businessman.' Hickman must have been thinking, so was Al Capone…

Returning to the relation between fetishism and crime, the Shoe Rapist case illustrates the intensely privatised fantasy, with its inner compulsions to apply a twisted ritual to both the offending itself and to the 'sacred' items that trigger the desire. Because this sickness is internalised, with a personal imagery and range of sensual arousal factors, the realisation – the actual making real – of the violence is equated with the attraction of the fetishistic object. That is, the woman is somehow an extension of what the shoe suggests, the pleasure it creates. Of course, the victim is never in any sense a part of the 'real' world for the attacker. He divorces the physical world from fantasy only when in the everyday role of, as in this case, print shop worker or taxi driver. The amazing aspect of all this for the layman, who simply reads the papers and forms opinions based on everyday experience and on concepts of 'normality' in behaviour, is how the two personalities can be present in the one person.

That is left for the experts to sort out. In the context of the daily run of serious crime in Britain now, the Shoe Rapist story will always represent that paradox: how the man in the smart suit, 'Mr Ordinary' who worked hard, could be a nocturnal predator who showed no respect for his victims and who treated them with savagery and amoral rage.

Chapter 20

Saturday Night Strangler
1973–2001

This is possibly the one story of DNA forensics that exemplifies the success of the profiling, even though the killer in this case was long dead. In 2001 police applied to the Home Office for permission to exhume the body of Joe Kappen, a man who had been a nightclub bouncer who had lived a few miles away from his victims, and who had been one of the suspects at the time. Samples from the girls' clothes were available, and Kappen, who died of lung cancer in 1990, was to prove to be the killer. It was a great achievement.

On 16 September 1973, the bodies of two teenage girls were found in Glamorgan, just a hundred yards apart, and they had died violently. They were both aged sixteen: Pauline Floyd of Longford, and Geraldine Hughes of Llandarcy. Only a few months previously, another sixteen-year-old had been found raped and murdered: Sandra Newton, her attacker killing her just six miles from the other girls. Pauline was found by an old man taking a morning walk, one by a farm road and the other in a wood, close to the playing fields at Llandarcy BP oil refinery. Then police found Geraldine shortly afterwards.

The resonance of those murders meant that on written accounts of the area in future years, as well as the refinery and other successful industry, and a very attractive village development, the murders became necessary references. One recent website account of the place says, 'The village is known notoriously, especially to local people, for the murders of schoolgirls...' *The Times* report made it clear that Roy Webb, the Assistant Chief Constable of South Wales, was sure that this was a double murder and the search was on for the killer.

The girls had been strangled with rope but no clothes had been taken or removed. Naturally, similarities were noted in comparison with the earlier Newton murder, as she also had been strangled, and with her own skirt, her body being discovered in an old pit culvert at Tonmawr. All three girls had gone missing after a night out.

Kappen had been spoken of in very negative terms at earlier stages of the inquiry. One man said, 'He was not a chap you would wish to fall out with,' and another, 'He could be a very nasty person, you wouldn't want to step on his toes.' But he was long gone when the digging began. There was a strong suspicion, before exhumation, that Kappen was the killer, and that he had also killed Maureen Mulcahy of Port Talbot in 1976. The modus operandi had been the same, Maureen being attacked and raped as she walked home from a night out. There had been numerous interviews with people who had known Kappen and a biographical account of him was put together, to help satisfy the curiosity about how such a man could live the dual life of family man and brutal psychopath.

He was born in 1941, in Port Talbot, in a large family; after the failure of his parents' marriage, he lived with his stepfather, and even at the young age of twelve he had been noticed by the forces of law, indulging in stealing cars, robbing gas meters and burglary. He was an habitual offender, always in prison for short stretches and then out again to thieve. Kappen had all kinds of jobs, from lorry driver to bouncer. A retired detective, Elwyn Wheadon, told the *Guardian* that Kappen was 'a man of a violent disposition, a Fagin-like character who sought out boys and girls to commit crimes on his behalf'. When Wheadon first came across him, it was after he had hurled a boy down some stairs. He was sure even then that Kappen was 'capable of anything'. He had been on social security, developed a fondness for drugs and for smoking. He was known to have chewed tobacco and to smoke twenty cigarettes a day. It was the familiar story of a man who was not really known or understood by anyone – a loner on the fringes of the community. He was seen in pubs, playing darts, but must have seemed destined to be alone, so his marriage to Christine Powell must have surprised many.

Christine recalled that he had been kind to her; she met him on a cold autumn day on the beach at Port Talbot. He bought her a hot chocolate. They later married and that lasted for eighteen years. He had a car, he worked out, and he was tall and handsome. She recalled his 'slate blue eyes' and Italian-like complexion. They had a child, and then once more, Kappen was in gaol, for burglary. When he came out of prison, he was the father of two children, the second being conceived on the day of his grandfather's funeral when he was allowed out of gaol. The man recalled by his wife in 2003 was a violent monster, striking and raping his own wife, and making her put up with his life of petty crime. She had to live with poverty and violence. But she never pressed charges against him.

In the murder hunt, his wife had provided an alibi, as she was in the habit of doing as she was a prisoner of his lifestyle of crime; but it was later realised how he had really escaped the net. Kappen had had his car, an Austin 1100, on blocks in the process of changing tyres, when first interviewed, but there had been a cast taken of the tyre tracks near the murder scenes. Kappen had been monitored at that visit as having no car out on the roads, but in fact he had been stopped in a routine stop and check by police the week after the murders. Computers would have found that cross-reference of course, but the anomaly was not seen and acted on at the time.

After they split up, Kappen lived with a local barmaid and they lived on the Baglan housing estate. Everything started coming to a stop when he was diagnosed with cancer, and from

1988 he was in a rapid decline.

The lead came when a match was done comparing the DNA on the clothing with that of Kappen's son Paul. The work then started at Goytre cemetery, the grave screened off, and the search for a closure reached its last stage. Jonathan Whitaker started the trawl after the swab records were gathered: he looked at the profiles put on the NDNAD and began to eliminate people. Whitaker said, 'We were looking for a father and getting to him by his son.' Paul Kappen, on the database, was found and the next step was to take DNA samples from Kappen's ex-wife, Christine Powell, and her daughter, then taking the female elements in the profile from the Kappen one (from his son). After two weeks, Colin Dark rang police to say, 'I think you've got your man.' DS Bethell heard the news, and told press that it was of course a marvellous thought, but that he needed to be absolutely certain of the facts when he told victims' families, 'The man in the grave is the man who killed your daughters.'

Permission was given, after five months, and the dig began on the hillside graveyard; Kappen was in a family grave, his coffin between his grandfather's and stepfather's. As the work was progressing, a storm broke. All three coffins had to be brought up, and Bethell has vivid memories of the occasion: 'The heavens opened and thunder and lightning started the like of which I have never seen... It was literally at the moment we came across the coffin of Kappen.' The coffins were taken to the mortuary and there was the body of the man who was almost certainly at that time the killer from 1973. Teeth were taken from the corpse, and also a femur, two sites of the best potential DNA samples to be taken. The bodies were put back in the ground and the tests began. It had been a grim operation, involving a whole team of forensic experts, including archaeologists and odontologists.

The results then came and the case was closed. But naturally, as with a number of killers whose stories are told in the earlier chapters here, it has been assumed that there will be other victims, so past cold cases have been checked again. Bethell told the press a few years ago, 'There have to be other rapes and unsolved murders that could be attributed to him.' In fact, other rapes that almost happened were recalled, such as one attack in which Kappen had done as early as 1964 – in that case a teenager had been taken onto a building site and would have been raped and strangled if she had not screamed for help. He had panicked and ran off. One man recalled that Kappen had a thrill 'going with young girls... even when he was forty-three.'

It may well have been Joe Kappen who picked up two girls near Neath in 1973. He drove to a quiet spot and said to the girl in the front seat, 'I know you want it.' There was then a desperate struggle and he punched the other girl in the face, but she had her long nails to thank for her life that day – she used them to pull up part of the door lock. Screams followed that as she got out, and luckily for the two girls, that disturbed a household not far off, and as they put on their house lights, he drove away. The car in question had been an Austin.

The DNA success in this case was down to the common sense approach of the scientists thinking that it was likely that the killer was local. As the report issued by the Forensic Science Service in 2005 stated: 'Following certain assumptions that families tend to live in the same area, and that criminality tends to run in families (and therefore a relative could be on the database) a search came up with 100 names. The intelligence was given to the local police, and combined with information they had, led to a local suspect being identified...'

As they say, the rest is history. It all sounds so straightforward, but of course the fact is that the case was revisited and closed because of a mix of logical deduction, educated guesses and rigorous and determined lab work on the profiles.

There is high drama in this story of an exhumation in a storm, a belated stare at the dead face of a killer and the pain of people alive who lost their loved ones or who suffered from the cruelty of this man who, in a thoroughly modern and scientific way 'spoke' from death. The familial DNA is undoubtedly a wonderfully powerful forensic tool, but there is always a down-side to these matters, as far as the police are concerned because they want their man when he can fight back, answer questions, be an opponent. As one officer said when the DNA results were given: 'To be honest I was disappointed. It was a let-down. You're not going to pull him in. It wasn't like arresting him and taking him to a court of law.'

What the Kappen case does show very plainly is that the double life of the psychopath is sometimes not quite so extreme in the contrasts of the two sides of the killer's nature. It is clear that the Kappen that Christine Powell found herself with in her marriage was a cruel, raging beast at home, and he raped in his own house as well as out on the road when he prowled for victims. Her account of him taking her forcefully on the day of his grandfather's funeral, while a prison officer waited in the house, says a great deal about his attitude to sex. In this instance, the beast in the man was never far away from the surface; unlike several other criminals in this case book, men who were able to make the Jekyll and Hyde template totally possible in their routines and working lives, Kappen was dangerous all of the time, but murderously dangerous some of the time.

Someone commented that for Kappen, predatory intent was combined with arrogance. That hints at why he was successful in applying a reign of terror; it also explains why he was successful in his 'normal' life. But it now seems that he always had a ligature and a knife on him. He needed to be on the move and alone to do his worst. That is a feature that doesn't fit a man who was a suspect in the case at one time – Fred West. No, this was a reign of terror that was far more predictable in its course of merciless cruelty. But at that time, thirty-six years ago, the technology for detecting the hellish outsiders of society was just not there.

Chapter 21

A Matter of Procedure
1990–1994

At the Court of Appeal in July 1994, one of the most important cases concerning the admissibility of DNA evidence took place. Stephen Cooke had been given a prison sentence of ten years for rape and six years for abduction running concurrently. The issue that enabled him to take his case to appeal was about DNA extracted from his hair, and whether the judge would allow this evidence.

This trial sheds light on the early difficulties of using DNA in the context of the Police and Criminal samples being taken. The success or failure of the appeal in some ways took second place to the whole subject of DNA samples from hair. In other words, it was part of the learning curve of DNA within the courts system.

The story began in April 1990 when a young woman was having a night out in Cheltenham; she met a group of men and one offered her a bottle of beer. She thought that they would walk with her but instead they left her and she started walking home alone. While walking, she was grabbed by a man and later recalled falling on some grass. She tied to fight back but she had not the strength, and the attacker's hand went over her mouth. She went unconscious and woke up to find herself in the back of a van, and she had no memory of being touched or handled, only that eventually the van pulled up and she was allowed out, and the man gave her some clothes.

The woman staggered into the doors of a nearby hospital. She was dazed and confused, and was holding a camisole around her body, her underclothes having been taken. Three nurses helped her, obviously seeing that she had been treated brutally: there were bruises and cuts on her body and her face was swollen. She must have looked as though she had been knocked over and savagely beaten up; she was wearing her jacket inside out, and held her tights in one hand. The attack had been quite near the hospital, as the lights there had caught her attention and she had walked towards them for help. It was discovered later that a couple were woken up by the noise of the van she had been in and that the man, a Mr Link, saw the car, giving a rough description. When he was then shown a number of pictures of vans, he picked out the van he thought was the one in question, but it was found that that van had no side sliding-door. That line of enquiry led nowhere, but at least it seemed possible that the attacker might have been prevented from doing something worse than rape.

Police came and she had a medical examination. Vaginal swabs were taken and the forensics team found semen, and that there had been sexual intercourse within the last twenty-four hours. There was semen on her camisole and this matched the samples taken in the vaginal swab. An interesting note on this testing, in the light of later cases, is that there was no semen left after this work for the defence lawyers to look at.

In June 1991, another woman was attacked in the town, and this time she was followed home and the assailant was bold enough to enter her home, with her parents sleeping close by, and attempt to rape the victim at knifepoint. Her screams woke her parents and the attacker ran off. When he was arrested, he was recognised by the victim in a line-up, and because she had been attentive when followed, she recalled some of the car number plate: this matched the van used by the man.

After this, Cooke had hair taken for testing and it was pulled, so that the root came with it. Earlier, after he returned from abroad a few months before this, he agreed to give a hair sample, but strangely, he took this himself – and it was cut. It will be recalled that DNA is only existent in the root follicles of hair. So the first sample, from cut hair, was useless for testing, while the second one, taken by forensic scientists, was perfect and gave them usable samples. A DNA profile was taken at the Chepstow Forensic Laboratory and Dr Dark compared that with the profile in the semen on the camisole and swab from the first attack.

This is the narrative behind the appeal court hearing. Cooke was arrested and charged in connexion with both attacks, so there were charges of rape and abduction facing him. He was acquitted at first, because the samples related only to the one attack. This had been recorded on a custody sheet. But of course there was enough forensic evidence to lead to another charge and trial for the other case in which the match had been made. It was a dramatic scene because the police were allowed to take the sample by force. When the sample was refused, the police made ready, fully attired in riot clothes, to enter his cell and forcibly take the hair; at this he relented and the sample was taken. That was when the DNA matches were done and found to be perfect. The forensic scientist, Dr Dark, said that the chances of the attacker being someone other than Cooke were 1.73 million. 'These findings indicate that the semen on the camisole and from the pooled swabs has come from Stephen Cooke.'

At the first trial the court refused to accept either of the samples from the hair. Everything hinged on the wording and interpretation of the Police and Criminal Evidence Act. It was eventually decided that the second sample was admissible. What then had to happen in order to convict Cooke was for the jury to be convinced by Dr Dark's account of the DNA evidence. Both topics were used to launch the appeal after conviction, when Cooke had been in prison for three years. At appeal, the argument was on these two issues: whether the procedure for taking the hair samples was condonable and whether the methods of giving the evidence to the jury were acceptable.

All this entailed a large amount of explanation about the DNA in hair. Once again, we have a case in which the expert witness, in this case a dermatologist, has to express complex matters in order to back up the nature of the DNA work. This was all done to try to achieve one result – that the samples were non-intimate in the terms of the 1984 Act. The questioning of the expert was done deftly and to the right purpose, including this interchange:

If it is live tissue you are wanting for DNA purposes, what are you trying to get?
WITNESS The inner sheath cells – next to the hair at the lower end...
Q That is material containing DNA?
WITNESS Indeed. Some of the cells will be already dead and will not contain that significant DNA.
Q But others will be living?
WITNESS Indeed...

It was all eventually successful, and the discussion had to sort out exactly what the behaviour of the police had been when they were ready to storm the man's cell. Was that an assault? Or did they have the powers to do that under the 1984 Act? Section 63(3) of that Act made it clear that the approach was allowed. It would not have been had the wanted hair been the man's pubic hair.

The other matter had nothing to do with DNA. It was about the judge's summing up at the original trial. He said about Cooke: 'I will mention that he told you he has a phobia about needles and that was said at the time, though it is not recorded. What was recorded was the answer I have reminded you of. He told you also that he refused a mouth sample, a saliva sample, because he thought that was disgusting.'

In short, the hair was taken because he had refused the usual buccal swab. The appeal court judge finished with the words: 'We find nothing in these additional grounds of appeal to cause us to reach any other conclusion than the verdict that was arrived at on admissible evidence...'

The Cooke case, then, is one that illustrates how, in the first few years of DNA evidence in court, the uneasy balance between police powers and the extraction of DNA was yet another learning curve. But in the end, the rapist and abductor went back to his cell. As with most of the cases here, there may well be backtracking going on to find other connexions, as with a *Crimewatch* appeal relating to an attack and rape in April 1990, an offence committed in daylight with people around. The pattern with attacks such as these done by Cooke is clearly that they will keep happening and the boldness will increase, so the danger increases. The contrast between the attacks discussed here – one in the street late at night and the second in the victim's home – shows that the excitement and the desperation in the features of the crimes were accelerating.

The drama here was in the court room as well as in the cell; the terror, however, was out on the streets, and once again, the skills of the forensic scientists resolved matters and put the aggressor behind bars. It was a matter of procedure and in the end the 'right' procedure was accepted and justice done.

Chapter 22

Freed After Twenty-Seven Years
Sean Hodgson
1982-2009

He was once thought to be the 'Crucifix Killer' but he was a sick man in a gaol who should not be there. As I write this he is being freed from prison and will no longer be called a killer. Science has liberated this complex man and put his name in the chronicles of miscarriages of justice.

The man's identity has always been a problem. The truth about him has always been a mystery. In 1982, *The Times* reported that he was 'Robert' and now he is 'Sean'. But from that very first report of the trial in connection with the murder of Teresa de Simone in Southampton in December, 1979, this has been a story about lies. The headline then was 'Man Tells Jury: I am a Liar.' Now, twenty-seven years later, this case is set to be a miscarriage of justice to equal the stories of Stefan Kiszko and Stephen Downing (the latter given a twenty-seven-year sentence and then being proved innocent).

The case also brings the importance of the Criminal Cases Review Commission centre stage and shows that DNA forensics is now just as capable of exonerating a person as helping to convict them. Of course, we now see the strangeness of the trial at Winchester Crown Court in 1982, when Hodgson in the dock

said, 'I would like to tell members of the jury I cannot go into
the witness box because I am a pathological liar.'

The story begins when Simone, a gas board clerk and part-
time barmaid, was attacked and killed in a car park in
Southampton. She was choked with a chain she wore – a chain
with a gold crucifix. At the time, Hodgson made a confession,
saying that he had murdered her when she found him asleep in
her car and caused panic as she screamed at the shock.
Hodgson's confession was made to a Roman Catholic priest. He
said that he had put his hand over her mouth to keep her quiet,
but then that led to her murder. There is a great deal of
vagueness in that, and questions concerning the gap between a
hand over the mouth and a forceful, intentional choking with a
chain. He had told the priest that the girl's image was 'haunting'
him.

The victim was just twenty-two, and had been sexually
assaulted. Her body was half-naked when found, and the
detective in charge of the case, DCS Harry Pilbeam of
Hampshire CID said that 'sex was the motive for the murder'.
The girl had lived in Shirley, at Reynolds Road.

The original trial took fifteen days, and there was a
unanimous verdict of guilty after a three-hour jury discussion.
The presiding judge, Mr Justice Sheldon said, 'It is a verdict
with which I entirely agree. I have no doubt whatsoever that you
were guilty of this appalling, horrible crime of killing that girl.'
That has to be one of the most deeply ironical statements ever
made by a judge in a criminal court. There was no appeal
allowed after that. But the complication in all this should have
been with regard to the fact that Hodgson had withdrawn his
confession and had pleaded not guilty. He had confessed to
hundreds of other crimes, including burglaries that did not exist.

Hodgson, now fifty-eight, grew up in the Tow Law area in the
North East, growing up in the Attlee estate, but leaving there
after the age of eleven. In the long years of imprisonment, he had
been outside the prison walls on just one occasion: to attend his

mother's funeral. Neighbours have told the press that Olive Hodgson 'Came from Ireland... and was a lovely woman. Jack was in the RAF in the war.' Jack, his father, is also dead, but he has two brothers and four sisters who still live in that area. Back in 1982, Hodgson's parents spoke to the *Northern Echo* and said that they were very doubtful about his guilt and could not understand why their son had made that confession to the priest while doing a stretch on a car-theft charge. It was all simply put down to 'attention-seeking'. At school, Hodgson was always in some kind of trouble; he was at Tow Law Junior and Infant School, near his home, but he started a life of crime when young and did his first stretch in a borstal.

But in 2008 a new legal team took over this case. Hampshire police were asked to review the evidence and to do some DNA testing. Hodgson had been most recently in Albany Prison on the Isle of Wight. While he was languishing there in the last few months, he had no idea that the DNA tests on materials preserved since the killing were to show that samples taken from the stored materials in the police archive did not match Hodgson's profile. The matter was then taken to the Criminal Cases Review Commission for urgent attention.

The Court of Appeal freed Hodgson on 18 March 2009. Julian Young, Hodgson's solicitor, commented: 'Will this open the floodgates? I would say anyone who believes that they have been wrongly convicted, and thinks DNA tests would help, should contact a lawyer immediately.' Of course this will open the floodgates. The national newspapers for offenders in prison, *Inside Time* and *Context*, regularly run features on the topic. Meanwhile, Hodgson faces the strange and possibly daunting experience of walking back into some kind of 'normal' life. But the questions now asked should be about the nature of his mental condition and of course, about the CCRC and DNA. His conviction has been ruled as 'unsafe' by the Lord Chief Justice, Lord Judge. The real killer has not been found, of course.

The CCRC will have to cope with plenty of other similar cases; after all, in 1982 there was no DNA testing available, and Hodgson's blood type was within the A or AB that marked the blood found at the crime scene – around one third of the male population are in that category. The contrast of that forensic detail by the side of DNA samples is staggeringly huge. But the facts of the trial and conviction at the time were plainly put by DCI McTavish, who said, 'Mr Hodgson was convicted by a jury on evidence which included his own admission to a clergyman, prison officers and police... There were also a number of other strands...'

The CCRC was set up in 1997 with the task of exposing wrongful convictions and putting right the failings of the criminal justice system. In 2007, the chairman told the press: 'Widespread dishonesty, impropriety and corruption within whole sections of police forces... I think are a thing of the past.' But he added that failings or dishonesty of individuals could 'never be eliminated'. So we have a watchdog and a supervisory organisation for cases such as Hodgson's. The man who became known as 'The Crucifix Killer' was no such thing, and the CCRC is what we rely on to ensure that we minimise the recurrence of these cases in the future. Between 1997 and 2007 the CCRC completed 8,500 case reviews. It deals with around a thousand cases a year. Only 4% of these tend to be reviewed, and there were 343 referrals made in that ten-year period. Of 292 cases heard at appeal from those referrals, 200 have been quashed.

A *Times* report made in 2007 argued that, 'The work by definition is labour-intensive and time-consuming. Caseworkers spend from thirty hours to four years on a case. Former lawyers, former police officers, court staff, they all have a knowledge of the justice system.' The success list includes such major stories as those of Derek Bentley, Timothy Evans, Sally Clark and Barry George. Other high profile cases are still pending. But in these days in which DNA testing is so easily done if storerooms and archives still have objects and materials, then matters may be righted. Naturally, in the cases of Bentley and Evans, those men went to the noose long before their innocence was proven. But for Hodgson and for others who will inevitably follow, DNA is on their side if they are innocent.

The categories of crimes most prominent in the CCRC files are, as Graham Zellick said in 2007, 'problem areas' and these are 'historic sex abuse cases, because the events occurred a long time before and there is a lack of corroborative evidence; expert evidence' and the *Guardian* reporter added, 'he questions the abilities of juries to cope in cases with complex expert testimony'.

As several of the foregoing cases in this book have highlighted, everything depends on the preserved material. Time and time again, clothes have been found in storerooms and cupboards, and by sheer good fortune on the part of the innocent, the testing has been possible. As a footnote to the Hodgson story, it has to be said that there must be a plea to the 'cold case' procedure in police forces about preservation of materials; it is not uncommon to read announcements in newspapers that some constabularies are ordering the removal of some cold case archives as part of cost-cutting exercises. It has to be hoped that the case of Sean Hodgson reminds any such 'economy measure' initiatives and the officers involved that such removal might keep an innocent person behind bars in time still to come.

Legal history shows that there has always been a proportion of innocent people behind bars; although it is a standard piece of humorous banter in gaols across the land that, 'Everyone in a cell is innocent of course…' I have had that said to me on several occasions while working in prisons. But the plain fact is that there are indeed innocent people serving sentences, and their voices are unheard because they are swallowed up by the general clamour for attention as convicted prisoners study their editions of Archbolds (guidelines on pleading and evidence)in the prison libraries, reading up on the laws of evidence and looking, as WC

Field did in the Bible 'for loopholes'.

The Hodgson case shows how the question of mental illness is placed in this context. Given the fact that a high proportion of convicted prisoners in our country are in some way mentally troubled, ranging from depression to paranoid schizophrenia, the time is long overdue when revisions and reviews should be made of cases within the period of those few years before DNA testing came into forensic use, and in the few years immediately after the Pitchfork and Melias cases.

Meanwhile, Sean Hodgson has to face a renewal of life, a life outside his pad and the prison walls. As many lifers will testify, that can be a more frightening and awesome experience than the thought of another day inside, and he will need all kinds of help and support. His 'unsafe' conviction is only the beginning of what must be hoped is a crime-free period for the rest of his life. His pathological lying, pseudologia fantastica, or mythomania, will have been understood in terms of its trajectory over his criminality and its timescale; at earlier stages, the lies will have been partially convincing, and the attention and limelight following that lying no doubt fuelled more lying. That has been a personality disorder for the man, and the attention he has had in early 2009 may not have been fully absorbed by him.

He will certainly have plenty of attention now, and his one 'big lie' that led to his conviction for the murder of Simone, has ironically led to his being the centre of media attention. As the DNA of the real killer from 1979 lies in the forensic archives, the hope goes on that more cases like Hodgson's will hit the headlines in the future. All the lying in the world cannot overturn what DNA testing tells us, and that fact remains the focus of hope for the innocent in prison cells today.

Chapter 23

Conclusions and Issues

In 1998, Jenny Ward wrote:

Since DNA was first used, different methods have evolved; so it isn't always possible to compare samples across time. Or from different labs using a different technique... There are other difficulties with comparison. What criteria do you use to decide that two profiles are identical? In physical fingerprinting, a rule gradually evolved that there had to be a sixteen point of resemblance for the fingerprints to count as identical...

This admirably expresses the doubts felt in the early years of the application of DNA profiles in forensics. But, as described in some of the previous chapters, today the situation is different: the courtroom problems with the use and expression of the arithmetic involved in explaining recurrence probabilities have been sorted out. There is now a power and a gravitas along with the presentation of DNA evidence and there has been more general understanding of the technology in legal quarters. Of course, the criminal is also aware of this and hence the debates on human rights as discussed in the introduction to the present work. What debates remain then?

The major focus here has to be the refusal of the British government to adhere to the European ruling on erasing DNA samples from the database in cases where the person in question is innocent of the alleged offence. In February 2009, it was announced that the Government planned to retain these samples. The *Guardian* reported that, 'The Government is planning to get around a European ruling that condemned Britain's retention of the DNA profiles of more than 800,000 innocent people by keeping the original samples used to create the database...'This clearly raises important civil liberties issues. The British database is the largest in the world, with five million entries. The barrister involved in the European case said: 'The European court has said that if the UK government wants to be a pioneer of the DNA database it will have to make a stronger case.'

Jack Straw has presented the argument in favour of this retention of samples, and he had in mind the Bill of Rights forthcoming in Britain. He wrote: 'And while the ends can never justify the means, our motives for seeking better protection for citizens from terrorism and crime are hardly ignoble. Those who cast myself and my colleagues as Orwellian drones engaged in some awful conspiracy planned in Whitehall basements not only overlook all this government's achievements, they cheapen the important debate about getting the balance right...'

But on the other hand, the *Guardian* also reported the case of a man from Hull who, when he was sixteen and at a fairground, put false coins into a machine and short-circuited the place. He was told that his details would only be kept until he was eighteen. Now, after serving twenty years in the Army, he has been blocked from a job working with children because that little misdemeanour is still on the record and he is on the database. There are thousands of similar cases to that. The oppositions here are between the argument that a comprehensive database, covering such minor cases as this, would also embrace the minority of very dangerous criminals who were at the very beginning of a long trajectory of criminal behaviour when the first minor charge was made. There will inevitably be the tiny percentage of psychopaths among that 800,000 population whose DNA is now kept – and retained illegally in terms of European law.

In terms of the practical applications of DNA work, a few major labs are now at work, rather than the initial number with, as Ward points out, their different conditions, so evidence and also the names and professional status of scientists have become familiar as the press and media have paid more attention to these matters. The only real discussion in the last few years in this respect has been with regard to Low Copy Numbers (as mentioned in Chapter 5). But in early 2008, the Caddy report led to the acceptance that very small samples of DNA evidence are safe to use in criminal prosecutions. Professor Brian Caddy from Strathclyde supervised this report, and asserted that there should be no wrongful convictions from LCN samples.

This came after the result of the Omagh bombing case in which Sean Hoey was acquitted of the murder of twenty-nine people in that bombing of 1998. The judge in that instance, Lord Justice Weir, ruled that the DNA material was not well collected and handled. That gave a shot in the arm to the forensics teams. The heart of the issue is that LCN traces, called 'touch DNA', is such that from only four or five cells samples can be taken. That would include for instance, someone picking up a gun and shooting it, although it had only been held for a few seconds. But the evidence from that source had also been used in the high-profile Peter Falconio trial and so it has been open to review, and now the Caddy report has dealt with the main problems.

Caddy made twenty-one recommendations: the main line of thought is that police gathering methods have to be free from contamination. That was the issue, it will be recalled, in the Molseed case when Castree was charged. But we now have a national agreement on how results from such tests have to be handled and interpreted. The result has been that Andrew Rennison, the forensic science regulator, has ruled that this science is safe. He commented in response to the report: 'However, there is clearly work to be done to develop a coherent standards framework that is transparent, accessible and used across all the facets of forensic science.' Nevertheless, there has been a hiatus in the application of LCN; in early 2008 the Association of Chief Police Officers in England and Wales said that there needed to be a suspension of its use until the CPS had reported on procedure. But the situation at present is that the CPS has given the red light, writing that LCN DNA 'should remain as potentially admissible evidence'.

Taking into consideration the timescale of the cases covered by the foregoing cases – from 1946 to 2009 – the conclusion most in mind has to be that the application of DNA profiling has been a silent revolution in the operations of investigation into serious crime; along with advances in forensic archaeology, it has plainly made biological science take centre stage after the limelight occupied by forensic profiling. Exactness has triumphed over instinct and empathy in that respect.

With a wider perspective, and with the focus on cold cases, it has to be said that the sad stories of these long-gone horrors keep making the headlines. Sometimes the case is closed by sheer chance or human nature, as in the 'voice from beyond the grave' in Manchester in 2008, when a long-standing Liverpool murder was apparently solved with a confession written after a man's death. Thirty-eight years after the murder of Lorraine Jacobs, in Liverpool, it seems that Harvey Richardson, who was a retired librarian aged seventy-seven, died and was buried; relatives went to tidy his room and they found a satchel with the confession inside. Richardson was not known to police; but after that finding, Merseyside Police started a cold case review.

This shows that chance and circumstance play a part in the resolution of long-standing cold cases; forensic science can speed up the process, but an element of luck tends to help. The conclusion drawn from the sheer number and scale of cold cases in Britain is that a prompt to re-open has to be hoped for any kind of lead that would bring in a placing of a DNA procedure. There are a number of examples in recent years that show the value of the investment in time and manpower in a cold case review. Perhaps one of the most typical has been Operation Phoenix in Newcastle. This arguably provides the template for the proper understanding of how DNA fits in with a large-scale revisiting of a long-standing crime.

Operation Phoenix in 2002 took DNA fingerprints in a number of cases from dusty old files; one of these related to the murder of an eleven-year-old who had been grabbed while waiting for a bus and taken to a park by a rapist. This happened back in 1981 and after a long and fruitless search the investigation came to a halt. But there were forty-one suspects when the case was looked at again in 2002 and it succeeded. DI Garry Dixon of Northumbria Police told the BBC, 'The actual feeling within the community was running very high as it was an eleven-year-old girl... As police officers you don't forget a case like this, you can carry one around with you for many years.'

But the evidence was reviewed, from all those years ago; there have been twelve convictions from Phoenix, and one of them was for this rape – a man called Wallace being linked and then charged. Dixon's comments on why the trawl succeeded are enlightening. He noted the range of commitment needed: 'Victims of crime have come forward and have been absolutely amazed that we are showing interest after so long... they have been hugely grateful.'

Operation Phoenix shows that three contributions are needed for cold case success, in addition to the scientific expertise: the will to work hard, undergoing a kind of detective archaeology; the finance to pay for the time, and co-operation from both members of the public and from victims or relatives of victims. In this case, the partnership involved was an operation with the Forensic Science Service, the Crown Prosecution Service and Victim Support. The convictions secured from the work include serial rape and indecent assault. Sentences given as a result include a double life sentence.

DI Dixon sums up the virtues of all this when he says, 'With changes in the law when any person is arrested they will be

sampled and I am positive that will have an impact.' The cases
described here support his statement, and although in the Lyon
and Aram cases the search is still on, one lesson has been
learned: the length of time is not a factor; as long as there are
cellular traces still present somewhere, there will be hope that
DNA profiles will be obtained. The LCN methods may be as far
as we can go with this, but that has proved to be a massively
successful weapon in the police armoury when cold cases
reopened again.

The issues and debates in this area of criminal investigation
will always be controversial; the Cooke case shows how difficult
the acquisition of a just outcome may be, and the fact that
eventually the criminal may be in his grave and beyond reach
adds another dimension to the sense of closure that is always
expressed in a cold case. It would not be too high a claim to say
that DNA in forensics has brought about a revolution in crime
investigation, and now that there is a conflict of interest between
the advocates of civil liberties and universal 'fingerprinting' on
the national database, the ruling from the Court of Human
Rights will have to be countered in some way and a compromise
found here in Britain. But familiarity lessens the sense of awe
and fear in what science has in terms of its capabilities in erasing
our sense of uniqueness. With the more general understanding
and acceptance of paternity testing, the criminal dimension will
perhaps not be seen as something smacking of a malevolent 'Big
Brother'.

To understand how far the science of applying DNA
fingerprinting within the legal processes of the criminal justice
system, we only have to consider the history of its acceptance in
court over the time span of the cases in the foregoing chapters.
There have been several phases in this: first the DNA material
was explained very carefully and introduced with caution and
hesitancy; then, as such expert witnesses were called began to
perform more consistently and their understanding of the
pitfalls of jargon and probabilities increased, there was a more

unified application. Then finally, with the streamlining of the forensics science services and a number of principal organisations involved, DNA evidence has become almost expected everywhere.

Of course, there is also the other side of the coin: miscarriage of justice. The Kiszco story has been important here because it was a massive presence in the media for so long, and the emotional appeal of the tragic fate of the innocent man affected more than the sympathies of those who knew the facts: it brought about a more urgent need for a revision of some aspects of police investigation. There are now extensive websites and popular publications on true crime and crime history that spend a lot of time compiling and describing cases of miscarriages of justice. One particularly telling example of this is in the publications and television programmes from Martin Young and Peter Hill called *Rough Justice*. These works were published or broadcast in the years immediately before the Pitchfork case and the arrival of DNA in forensics. *Rough Justice* and *More Rough Justice* appeared in 1983 and 1985 respectively; one statement made in the first book tells us exactly what DNA can and will achieve in elimination. The authors wrote:

> *A young man was sentenced to four years for sexual assault. Three independent witnesses and the girl herself testified that the assailant was around five feet seven to nine inches tall, slimly built and wearing blue denim jeans. The man sent to jail is six feet tall, weighed fourteen and half stones at the time of the crime and did not own any blue denim clothes. Today he has served nine years and is in Broadmoor Mental Hospital, detained partly because he will not confess that he was guilty of the original crime.*

If we go further back, into the years of capital punishment, it could be pointed out that Arthur Koestler and Leslie Hale wrote two books in the 1960s about notorious and less well-known cases of innocent people going to the gallows, and several cases in doubt after later investigation.

In fact, what is apparent from these cases and the miscarriages of justice associated with some of them is the media perspective. When the tabloids create distortions and misconceptions about the 'science' of forensics – profiling as much as biological forensic work – the repercussions of presenting the public with often dangerous falsifications and misguided statements are felt everywhere. In the Molseed case, this is perhaps most seriously apparent.

DNA has, above all else, removed the uncertainty and the possibility of severe mistakes potentially made by well-meaning people caught in the inner workings of a complex and often very rigid judicial system. While there is still a very important place for such professionals as forensic botanists and archaeologists, ear-print specialists and handwriting experts, DNA has proved to be the ultimate dispenser of certainty in these affairs, and only errors from the human element in police investigation will puncture that secure vessel and make regrettable judicial leaks.

Once again, Shakespeare has the words for this: Foul deeds will rise/ though all the earth o'erwhelm them/ to men's eyes. (Hamlet)

Bibliography and Sources

Books

Ainsworth, Peter B *Offender Profiling and Crime Analysis* (Willan, 2001)

Bass, Dr Bill, and Jefferson, John *Beyond the Body Farm* (Quercus, 2008)

Bell, Colin *The Murderer Hunters: the detectives' inside stories* (Deutsch, 2002)

Bresler, *Fenton Scales of Justice* (Weidenfeld and Nicolson, 1973)

Britton, Paul *Picking Up the Pieces* (Corgi, 2001)

Britton, Paul *The Jigsaw Man* (Corgi, 1997)

Butler, J M Forensic *DNA Typing* (Academic Press, 2001)

Canter, David *Mapping Murder* (Virgin, 2003)

Douglas, John and Olshaker, Mark *Mindhunter: inside the FBI serial crime unit* (Arrow Books, 2006)

Fielder, Mike *Killer on the Loose: the inside story of the Rachel Nickell murder investigation* (Blake, 1994)

Godwin, John *Killers Unknown* (Herbert Jenkins, 1960)

Hill, Peter and Young, Martin *Rough Justice* (Ariel, 1983)

Hill, Peter and Young, Martin *More Rough Justice* (Penguin, 1985)

Hunter, John et alia *Studies in Crime: An Introduction to Forensic Archaeology* (Routledge, 1997)

Krawczak, M and Schmidtke, J *DNA Fingerprinting* (Oxford, 1994)

Lane, Brian *The Encyclopaedia of Forensic Science* (Headline, 1992)

Lyle, D P *Forensics* (Writers' Digest, 2008)

Moore, Pete *The Forensics Handbook* (Eye Books, 2004)

Odell, R *Landmarks in 20th Century Murder* (London, 1995)

Putwain, David, and Sammons, Aidan *Psychology and Crime* (Routledge, 2004)

Saferstein, R Criminalistics – *An Introduction to Forensic Science* (Prentice Hall, 1991)

Taylor, Bernard and Knight, Stephen *Perfect Murder: a century of unsolved homicides* (Collins, 1988)

Vronsky, Peter *Serial Killers: the method and madness of monsters* (Berkley Books, 2004)

Ward, Jenny *Crimebusting: breakthroughs in forensic science* (Blandford, 1998)

White, PC (ed) *Crime Scene to Court, the essentials of forensic science* (Royal Society of Chemistry, 2004)

Wilson, David *Serial Killers: hunting Britons and their victims 1960-2006* (Waterside Press, 2007)

Journals and Legal Publications

Legal History

Police Review

Reports of the Courts of Appeal (Sweet and Maxwell, various)

Science and Justice

Articles

Bono, JP 'The Forensic Scientist in the Judicial System' *Journal of Police Science and Administration*, Vol. 9 no.2 pp.160-166

Canter, David 'We Need Smarter Police Who are Science Savvy' *The Times* 19 Dec 2008

Daeid N 'DNA - What Next?' Science and Justice No.47 (2007)

Edwards, Richard 'Will We Ever Get Inside the Criminal Mind?' *Daily Telegraph* 19 Dec 2008

Freckelton, IR *The Trial of the Expert: a study of expert evidence and forensic experts* (Oxford, 1987)

Jeffreys, A et alia 'Hypervariable Minisatellite Regions in Human DNA' *Science and Public Affairs*, 7 March 1985 p.67

Robins, John 'Miscarriages of Justice: are the bad old days returning? *Times Law Supplement* 16 October 2008

Websites and Archival Resources

BBC News Channel: news.bbc.co.uk
www. Cps.gov.uk
www.forensic.gov.uk/forensic
www.genewatch.org
www.guardian.co.uk
www.homeoffice.gov.uk/science-research
www.independent.ie/national-news
Jill Dando Institute of Crime Science:
www.jdi.ucl.ac.uk/crime_mapping
www.physorg.com/news
http://news.scotsman
www.telegraph.co.uk
www.thisisbristol.co.uk
The Times Digital Archive
www.tribune.ie/news
www.viewzone.com/oetzi

Acknowledgements

Many people and organisations helped with the research for this book. Thanks go to Newsquest and to David Stock for permission to use the pictures from the Keith Lyon case; Ken Lussey at Undiscovered Scotland for the use of the *World's End* image; Catherine Townsend at Save Britain's Heritage for the use of the Carlton Hayes picture, and Vicki Schofield for the illustrations. Also due for some thanks are Cathy White, Andy Owens and Carl White. Finally, Brian Elliott, the series editor, has been, as usual, a great support in the writing process. For the Salt's Mill picture, thanks go to saltairevillage.com

Writing this book required a considerable amount of technical support. For help with the necessary scientific knowledge required for the project, thanks go to Helen Anderson, who read the manuscript and suggested clarifications.

Glossary of Terms

Note: this is merely a selected grouping of terms and references. The entries here are made simply to give the reader a quick reference while reading the text, to add extra clarification. For a fuller explanation, the trail leads to specialist textbooks of course. But also recommended is Brian Lane's reference work (see Bibliography). Admittedly, full and detailed explanations are likely to destroy the interest, so this information is not more complex than the average 'true crime' feature. Hopefully, the facts will lead to further enquiry.

Autorad
In a tagged probe, there is radioactivity, and this is used to expose film, and that film is where the patterns are seen that make up the 'fingerprint' of the individual.

Chromosome
The structure made up of gene units.

DNA
Deoxyribonucleic acid, a molecule that encodes an individual's genetic profile. Samples are taken, mostly from blood, saliva, semen, skin, teeth and hair. The DNA molecule is a polymer – a long line of repeating pieces, and these are the bases. It is double stranded, hence the term 'double helix' describing the form of the bases in their pairs (see illustration 1). This is a spiral – shaped structure, looking like a ladder that has been twisted around.

Forensic Science Service

Since 2005, the FSS has been a government-owned company, providing quick responses for demand in police investigation. Its main tasks are to be the main provider of forensic services to the police and to develop new data initiatives such as the National Firearms Forensic Database (2003) and the Footwear Intelligence Technology (FIT) database – the latter being the first online footwear coding and detection management system, created in 2007. It played a major role in the creation of the first DNA database in 1995. It also produces publications and case studies and gives a service of information and new research for the media. See www.forensic.gov.uk

Genes

Units of DNA, the fundamental units of heredity.

Genome

This is a word referring to the total DNA in one single cell. Each individual has six billion bases and it is the varying sequences of these base pairs that form the DNA profile.

Junk DNA

The non-encoded elements in the genes.

Location of DNA

Although there is DNA in every tissue and fluid in the body, the substances obviously of most interest in a crime scene will be saliva, semen, urine, bone, teeth and hair. Semen, mentioned in many of the cases in this book, has DNA in the spermatozoa, but if a person has no sperm, then there will be no DNA. The seminal fluid, moving along the urethra, leaves cells with the DNA so this is one reason why, in some of the foregoing sexual assault cases, the 'sticky strips' taken and kept in the lab may be useful after so many years. The cells from the fluid have been 'frozen in time.'

Hair, as mentioned in two of the cases here, only provides DNA if the follicles have been taken with the hair strands. But the hair strand does have mitochondrial DNA.

In bone there are osteocytes where the DNA is found (see the story of Oetzi in Chapter 2). This material is sealed within those cell units for thousands of years, thus explaining why forensic archaeology and DNA sampling go closely together in many long-standing cold case research studies.

The buccal swab, mentioned regularly in the cases here, takes saliva, and although saliva itself has no cells, there are epithelial cells lining the salivary ducts in the mouth, and these cells contain DNA.

Low Copy Number

The term used when work is done in the lab on degraded, poor quality material. The decrease in quality may be caused by heat, decay or even by chemicals. See the 'World's End' case for the issues around this.

Mitochondrial DNA

A smaller molecule with over 16,000 base pairs, contrasted with the billions in the nucleus where DNA is found. mDNA changes or degenerates only very gradually, hence the discussion of the Crippen case (see Introduction).

NDNAD

The National DNA Database. When a suspect is arrested, the police have the powers to take a buccal swab (as things stand now) This is a 'CJ sample' – a Criminal Justice sample. Hence the issue of why these are kept when suspects are not later charged. There is also a Scottish DNA database, in Dundee. The British database has four million samples. But at the time of writing (2008) it looks as though European legislation may change all this.

Nitrogenous bases

Molecules forming the string of components, and just four of these bases play a part in the production of DNA: Guanine, Cytocine, Thymine and Adenine. All life is produced from these four molecules.

Pattern Matching
The gel used in the testing falls into columns or 'lanes' and these move to form separate lines and patterns. When the columns made in this way are matched by comparing the two samples, pattern matching has been applied to find similarities.

Polymorphism
Literally meaning, 'having many forms' – these are certain areas of a long DNA molecule

Proteases
These are enzymes that break down proteins – but they do not harm the DNA material.

Y-Chromosomal DNA
This is the DNA found only in males. By testing repeat sequences, common ancestry in males can be ascertained using this source. Of course, the use of this testing in genealogy is a massive growth area in DNA profiling.

INDEX